TMacKay

GENERAL SEMANTICS AND THE SOCIAL SCIENCES

BY THE SAME AUTHOR:

Contemporary Papers on Social Change and the Administrative Process

GENERAL SEMANTICS AND THE SOCIAL SCIENCES

REFLECTIONS AND NEW DIRECTIONS

by

Dr. WILLIAM J. WILLIAMS

Assistant Professor,
School of Public Administration
University of Southern California

Philosophical Library

New York

15 East 40 Street, New York, New York 10016

Library of Congress Catalog Card No. 71-155970
SBN 8022-2055-X

Printed in the United States of America

DEDICATION

This book is respectfully dedicated to my teacher, mentor, associate and friend, Dr. J. Samuel Bois, who is the leading theoretician in the field of Modern General Semantics, up-to-date epistemology and the father of the new discipline of epistemics.

And, to my two daughters, Morgan and Paige. Hopefully, the forerunners of a new direction.

FOREWORD

'The future has already begun,' wrote Robert Jungk a few years ago.

He was right: the physical sciences and the technology they had made possible were the beginnings of our world of tomorrow, the world of instantaneous communication, of freedom from gravity, of nuclear energy beyond dreams.

When it comes to the sciences of man and their application, we try to peep into a future apparently surrounded with a screen of mystery. We have invented utopias, from Thomas Moore and Jonathan Swift to Burrhus F. Skinner and Aldous Huxley, putting in an invented environment men and women who look very much like men and women as we know them.

Why not take Robert Jungk's viewpoint and look around, in what is actually happening in our world of humans, so as to discover the emerging features of the real future we have already entered? Gardner Murphy spoke of a 'third human nature' that he claimed is in the making. Lynn White, Jr. states that we are not only heirs of the past, but mutants as well. Are there, growing here and there, among the weeds of our cultural field, a few more civilized stems breaking out of the accumulated dirt and humus and showing promise of an unexpected crop of flowers and fruit as yet unknown? Can we detect living indicators of a new face of the earth, transformed by the action of a breed of human beings different from the 'old human nature,' self-centered, aggressive, obeying the territorial imperative and no better than a naked ape?

Yes, indeed, we can see these promising indicators, if we just take off the cloudy glasses of our rudimental culture and look around in fresh awareness. There are mutants among us;

the third human nature is taking shape right under our eyes.

We see it in the young generation, not only in the hippies and the flower children whose promising growth is still partly buried in the decaying remnants of the past; we see it in the generation that is already entering adulthood and adopting a more definite code of values translated in vigorous activities. Within the limited range of my personal observations I see it in the Peace Corps and the Vista volunteers who bring back from their experience an orientation of service and help for their fellowmen. I see it in the newly formed Campus Committee to Bridge the Gap, an organization of over 1,000 students that meet the older generation in friendly dialogues. I saw it recently in an experimental college, Johnston in Redlands, where students take the responsibility for their own education under the non-authoritarian guidance of learned returnees from the Peace Corps or similar experiences. I see it in the Ralph Nader raiders who penetrate the very vitals of our governmental bureaucracy and corporate frankensteins to inject into them the invigorating sap of humanness. I see it in these young attorneys who demand of law firms which they enter the freedom to serve their underprivileged brothers and sisters within the time allotted to standard professional pursuits. I see it in artists like Gary David who makes in the most advanced style of music, enjoyed in night clubs of high repute, the Sound of Feeling for transcendent values.

I see it in these pages where Bill Williams recites the tale of his personal odyssey from the black-white confrontation imposed upon his generation by our either-or culture to the transcending view of the human family, black, white, yellow, brown or red, in which all are yearning for a new dispensation, for a better world where they can all live proud of their differences and willing to share them in a common endeavor.

This coming generation not only has budding activists, public minded teachers and creative artists. It has its own scholars as well. Dr. William Williams is one. It was my privilege to witness his bursting development once the pressure of his talents and deeply felt values was released, thanks to the techniques made available by the time-binding wisdom of the great minds of our Western tradition. I had found that wisdom channelized within the recently traced borders of a system proposed one generation ago by Alfred Korzybski, and labelled tentatively by him General Semantics. Working together we dug a wider channel for the flow of that age-long wisdom, welcoming into it as tributaries the contributions of the sciences we were professionally engaged in.

I feel a personal pride and satisfaction in recommending these papers to a publisher, and through this to a reading public that is ready for them. The style is vastly different from mine, and why not? In my bad critical moods, I would call it a typical sample of 'academese,' the pompous stuffing of a simple mental model you want to appear big and important. But is the simplicity and the directness that I prize so highly the better kind of style? Could it be nothing but a conditioning of mine, that was instilled into me years ago and of which I am blandly conscious? Perhaps it is.

There are cases where simplicity is over-simplification. It may be distortion, reduction to a lower order of existence. It may also be too rapid an ascent to a stratospheric level of abstraction, so far away from the gravitation of common experience that very few are those who can sense its relevance to the situations they are facing.

Bill flies at an intermediate level, within the clouds of uncertainty and tossed about by the hurricanes of clashing opinions and purposes. I respect his style. I like his daring as he flies through the eye of the storm. I see emerging from his pen statements that no one has been able to structure as well as he does when he describes the sequence from grammar to general semantics in the following lines:

> Grammar deals with word-to-word relations. It teaches how to put words together into a sentence. It is not interested in how sentences are related to each other or how they are related to facts. Logic goes further. To a logician sentences are assertions, and he is interested in relations between as-

sertions. . . . For the logician words need not have any meaning except as defined by other words, and the assertions need not have any relation to the world of fact. The semanticist goes further than the logician. To him words and assertions have meaning only if they are related operationally to referents. The semanticist defines not only validity (as the logician does) but also the truth. The General Semanticist goes the furthest. He deals not only with words, assertions, and their referents in nature, but also with their effects on human behavior. For a general Semanticist, communication is not merely words in proper order, properly inflected, or assertions in proper relation to each other or in proper relation to referents, but all of these together, with the chain of fact to nervous system to language to nervous system to action.

The man who wrote this knows where he is at, and he feels his way with steady steps into the future he is structuring as he goes. With men like him the future that I see dawning upon the world is a future devoid of threats and full of promises. These promises are in gestation within the creative unit made of the brain, heart, and soul of the like of him. They will out in due time, I know. And we, the members of a previous generation who have kept the faith in the evolutionary urge that works incessantly to make men more human, feel good to participate in our own way in their enterprise of transforming themselves and the world in which we all live.

J. Samuel Bois, Ph. D.

July 22, 1970

TABLE OF CONTENTS

PREFACE

General Semantics And the Social Sciences: Reflections and New Directions offers brave optimism for the "change artist" who desires and promotes (intellectually-practically) growth and progress in the direction towards more human and creative humans.

Dr. Williams' theories apply to any "system", not just Public Administration. Not only does he afford insights into the special problems facing the new Public Administrator but his "theoretical overarching framework" provides valuable information for those involved in and with racial and social conflict, personal relationships, and so on, on a world-wide basis.

As J. S. Bois' works may be read and re-read, each time obtaining new dimensional implications, so follows Dr. Williams' treatise. He treads into the unknown, creating pathways and clearings in the jungle of the third generation general semanticists. He says, for example, in one instance:

> The One Man Theory holds that those who would like to bring about major changes must adopt first of all a relativistic view rather than an absolutist view. This view must tie our assumptions, frameworks and personal constructs to modern epistemology in a way that enables us to build a process that is in keeping with the process of the world and the cultural and automatic epistemic changes that are taking place. This is the beginning of a difference which makes a difference a *difference*.

Dr. Williams is *only* "one" time-binder, but we certainly cannot view his contributions to the world of humans as an additive affair, for his contributions may well be the difference that makes a difference a *difference!*

Mark C. Liebig
Institute of General Semantics
University of Denver
August 1970

ACKNOWLEDGMENTS

I am grateful to Mark Liebig for reading my manuscript and giving me an honest reaction. I am grateful to members of the USC School of Public Administration faculty and administration for their encouragement.

I am grateful to Dr. Bois for his encouragements and criticisms.

I am grateful to Alice Thibodeaux, our School of Public Administration executive secretary, for her support in making the manuscript available in mimeograph form.

I am grateful to Carl Bellone for his critical comments, encouragement and friendship.

My biggest booster, morale builder and loyal friend, Irene Yasutake, a critic, reader, and searcher for the right publisher.

There are others too numerous to mention in this short space. Please know that I appreciated and received with gratitude the encouragement and support.

INTRODUCTION

Through the years, and especially since Woodrow Wilson wrote his treatise on the study of Public Administration, Goodnow, his book on Politics and Administration, and the introduction of the Scientific Management Movement by Frederick Taylor, we were involved in a controversy as to whether public administration is an art or science. Waldo, Simon, and Gulick have contended that public administration was in the process of becoming a science. Charles Beard, however, contended that public administration was a science by virtue of the fact that systematic data has been collected. Others have contended that it has a scientific aspect and in retrospect the latter tend to separate the two. I contend that not only are they related and part and parcel of one another and inseparable, but it is undesirable to do so, except for analytical reasons. Regardless, analysis is done with language, whether analytic or synthetic.

My point then, whether a discipline is scientific or unscientific, depends upon the language used. Consequently, if the language is more scientific, as Bertrand Russell contends in his "Theory of Types," the assumptions drawn from macroscopic, sub-macroscopic, microscopic and sub-microscopic data will be easier to validate by referring them back to the events. This inheres in public administration: the field does not become scientific by eliminating the art i.e. hunches, feelings and attitudes, but by improving the quality of the art i.e., feelings, hunches, attitudes, by the use of a more scientific language.

At present time we do not bother ourselves with whether or not it is an art or science, we just seem to be carried by the tide and the need for more study and how to make the discipline more relevant to those in need of a more sophisticated approach to problem solving.

It seems to me, that more than anything else, at this time, we are in need of direction and a systematic way to determine the direction and the field as a process.

This brings us to the critical question of methodology and a sound theoretical base for automatically providing process and need direction. These papers are about methodology and a theoretical base. I do address the question of scientific but only as a lead in to a discussion about a process which takes us into the arena of the 'new scientific spirit.' The assumption being that we are already scientific and have always been; but, how do we assume the 'modern' scientific approach? In other words how do we move from the world of Newton to the world of Einstein and Planck, in the social sciences and social and public administration.

In answering this how question we begin with certain assumptions; a few are:

1. It is the contention that administrators operate automatically from a series of value assumptions within an overarching theoretical framework derived from some kind of base.

2. It is the second contention that in order to make an impact on policy, priorities and social directions, it is necessary for the administrator to work within an overarching theoretical framework derived from an epistemological base which speaks to the epistemic process (so called natural cultural process) of the world which inevitably affects the historical process. The former can be compared to the thalamic (silent) part of the brain and the other the cortical (speakable) and the 'Natural formative Tendency of the World.'

3. The third contention is that there is methodology which will enable us to work with the administrator on an organism-as-a-whole and non-elementalistic way. That is, we can work with what the administrator is, what he ought to be and what he might become by relating to a certain kind of process. That process is the Modern General Semantics Epistemological process which can be referred to as the language dimension of

modern epistemology; or, how we deal with our overarching theoretical framework which gives form to our action and which is always with us and is automatic.

4. The fourth contention contained in the papers among other things, is that the 'how to do' emerges, from the well defined 'what' of the situation. It is a sub-contention that the process and methodology move us to the position of developing our own creative decisions in particular case situations i.e., the process enables us to develop a systematic process, personal constructs and vehicles for action. Thus, improving our decision-making, self-management and overall effectiveness.

5. It is the fifth contention that behavior is pretty much predetermined in each situation and that pre-determination can be altered and made to work in keeping with a process of survival and living.

These writings are structural in nature and can be used by social scientists in general — including philosophers, psychoanalysts, social psychologists, business administrators, economists, etc. They happen to have a public administration substantive base, in small part, because I happen to be vehicling in the field of public administration.

These writings emerged out of a necessity to give coherence and direction for myself and my students who are utilizing the Modern General Semantics Epistemological process as a base and a procedural frame of reference.

Let me take a quote from a memorandum directed to the Director of our School of Public Administration from a group of our graduate students who were commenting on the processes that were taking place in my classes. I believe this says what I have tried to say much better than I ever could:

> The very real significance of these *writings* may be the fact that they go beyond the traditional management and organization theory and begin to prepare the future administrator for the rest of the world, of people and their interrelationships (transactions) one with the other and with their organizational and social environment. . . . It was

in Dr. Williams' classes we began to feel and to focus on the administrator, not only as a possessor of the tools of his trade, but as a dynamic force in his total environment where action reflects how well prepared he is to manage himself and to make that meaningful difference, a difference that makes a difference.

In a time of dramatic change we must develop a theoretical framework which will enable us to manage, direct, lead, and design blueprints for radical change.

We, in the social sciences, in the world of education and in particular public administration are called upon to assume leadership — to become involved in social conflict and change. We are called upon to develop a new methodology. We have come to the conclusion that our present methodology does not provide proper direction and courage. We are hamstrung with frames of reference and constructs that do not stand the test of time, and we operate with them unconsciously.

A parallel assumption is that since we do operate with some kind of frame of reference, why not operate with one that is in line with not only the survival order of the world, but can move humankind to the level of living and make him an effective time-binder which would necessarily have an impact on man's future development and progress. It is a subsidiary assumption that modern General Semantics epistemology will enable us to radically revise our constructs and provide us with the kind of process that will stand the test of time, revamp our obsolete notions, direct our energies in keeping with effective action, and enable us to operate in the best interest of humankind.

The General Semantics epistemological process in addition to providing us with tools and techniques to be applied in the re-education of groups, also provides us with a personal understanding which gives substance to the one man theory.

(One man can be a difference which makes a difference a *difference.*) The deep understanding is a rich resource for supplying confidence and courage, which are preludes to action.

We, in the social sciences, public administration, and education in general, are being requested to supply those who look to us with a meaning for life. It throws us immediately and directly into the depth of psychological, philosophical and epistemological concerns. Our professions confronted with such a problem may be well driven into a corner unless we ready ourselves to cope with the situation. We must, in addition to technical concerns, be concerned with spiritual distress and moral leadership coupled with "scientific methodology." The General Semantics epistemological process provides us with the opportunity. Thus, the reasons for adopting this methodology.

The third phase of the Scientific Revolution (conceptual cultural revolution) is systemic rather than local or isolated. It implies changes in society's operation and organization as profound as those that accompanied the suppression of agricultural production by the Industrial Revolution. It implies the introduction of widespread planning; the planning of not only economic institutions but cultural and scientific development; it implies the need for political integration of the world in some form of world order; it implies a change in the world's conception of work and the proper occupation of humankind. The organization of human culture is headed toward fundamental change, even the factors determining who shall assume leadership will undergo change. The summary of such matters points to the fact that the cultural revolution we are undergoing is truly systemic.

The genetic endowment, food supply, air and communication systems are as basic now as pursuits of life, liberty and happiness. The time is coming when the former, also, will become a part of political control, scientifically-artistically administered on a world wide scale. One of the most fundamental and insistent demands is that these affairs must be administered scientifically; this is different from the substantive employment of science to achieve a political end: Calling upon physics to produce a bomb, and chemistry to produce defoliants are examples of the latter. The procedures of science must replace the procedures of government.

While politics and administration possess the qualities of an art, new challenges such as the rapidity of social change, the resolution of social conflict, the complexity of modern administration, the image-building of today's politics, and almost overpowering multi-dimensional nature of our nation's societal problems work to make public management in the present century an increasingly complex science. The leaders of the next century will need thorough training in the Modern epistemological methodology of the future. We must develop a "scientifically artistic" approach.

We are in the midst of a cultural transformation and must become politically mature enough to deal with it. The old is at war with the new. Harvey Wheeler in his book *Democracy in a Revolutionary Era* (p. 155) says and I paraphrase: There are periods characterized by two fundamentally different cultural systems that exist simultaneously and are difficult to reconcile because they are dualistic and are at war with each other. It is the old against the new. The resulting conflicts penetrate every element of the social order. Dr. J. Samuel Bois in *Breeds of Men,* and again I paraphrase, says that at a given time a certain epistemic (Cultural) process is in motion and it is ahead of the historical process and unless the historical process is brought in line, "deep," "unrealistic" conflicts ensue. Our task is to develop processes for making this possible.

Both Wheeler and Bois agree on the kind of direction we should pursue. In many ways the direction they describe, ties in with the process I have tried to develop in the papers contained in this book. However, what I have said should only be considered a beginning. We must continue developing, the process I have outlined is a personal one and can enable all of us to develop our own from this one. And, most of all enable us to establish a direction, a methodology that may be similar to the conceptual cultural scientific processes taking place. More than that, a philosophical commitment and construct that will *stand the test of time.*

A conceptual tool serving as a backdrop to the overarching process I talk about is the concept of self management inherent in Dr. J. Samuel Bois' modern General Semantics epistemological process which is important and significant to social change, group-wise as well as individually. For example an essay by Sergi Mallet "Bureaucracy and Technocracy in the Socialist Countries," in *Socialist Revolution,* May-June, 1970 elaborates on the point, he says in essence: There is a contrast to be made between the concept of self-management and bureaucracy or administrative management. The latter belongs to the area of the means and most of the time our reforms, revolutions, or changes are translated in terms of administrative management. I infer from what he said, overall, that if we were to adopt the concept of self-management as we begin to attempt to implement our programs, we would be addressing ourselves to a cultural and social revolutionary growth which would give way to 'egalitarian cooperation.' Also, it addresses the process of a wider and more viable popular alternative to a state monopoly which enables the process to actualize man's actions — thus the concept of self-management. In the papers herein, I have talked of 'individual' self-management as it is implicit in the modern General Semantics epistemological process without relating it to the broader implications of what it holds for social change, social action, and future societal direction. This area requires more research and study. It is an example of how a simple concept changes our perceptions, and our direction and eventually the kind of actions we take.

Self-management can lead us to collective decision making. The $self_1$, $self_2$, $self_3$ can be easily applied in structural analysis of what the world is doing or what a nation is all about. It is related to self-reflexiveness and multiordinality. It enables a nation in process — to look at itself. It is a transference of individual self-awareness to group, national and world self-awareness, with the initiative for this lodged within the province of the individual and group concept. It ties in well with the one man theory and a difference which makes a difference a *difference.* The mere adoption and articulation by one individual in a sensitive and image-making position is enough to re-direct a course of action.

The self-awareness is a part of self-management Bois talks about and the self-consciousness Boulding talks about. And, the application is inherent in the modern General Semantics epistemological process.

The papers, herein, speak to expansion of an individual's personal equation, value system, and world view as a necessary prelude to being an effective organizational and societal change agent. In this light, change becomes a process of growth. The public administrator we are talking about, must have a change orientation and be a confident leader and innovator able to fuse man's creativity with the functional necessities of an organization's task.

Implications of social change, conflict resolution, self-renewal, general semantics, non-Aristotelian logic, and intergroup conflict are a part of these papers. Theories of organization and management are viewed in terms of how men can creatively use the process to bring about a more human condition for society. I view organizations as vehicles for change rather than as inhibitors of growth and development. Values and the relationship of our personal institutional positions must be examined in terms of emerging cultural factors brought to the surface by our Modern General Semantics Epistemological Framework.

I submit that man must confront himself and his values and move to the level of action. This enables great flexibility in translating personal values and skills into viable strategies of action in social administration.

The process moves us toward a unified theory of social and public administration.

The issues with which I am concerned are both theory finding and theory using. The one I am not concerned with at this point is hypothesis testing or validation.

The underlying theme is that a human being in order to be a good scientist, a good social scientist, a good administrator or an excellent leader must become a person, a human being, and an integrated person committed to the betterment of the human condition; and involved in a process that speaks to living and not just to survival — plants survive, animals occupy space and humankind lives.

William J. Williams
Assistant Professor
School of Public Administration
University of Southern California

CHAPTER I

PHENOMENOLOGY AND GENERAL SEMANTICS

Position Paper Number One

The "New" Public Administration

This is the first of several position papers to be developed by me on the subject of the "new" Public Administration. The paper is for internal consumption only at the present time. The first paper is devoted to a superficial analysis of phenomenology and General Semantics — a comparison, if you will, of several differences and similarities; this, hopefully, will establish somewhat a basis for application to Public Administration. This tack is taken, at this time, because in certain quarters some are seeking to apply phenomenology as I am attempting to apply General Semantics. This kind of discussion is necessary as our philosophies will determine, to some extent, the direction and models for Public Administration.

I equate what little I know of phenomenology with the abduction process. As I understand it, the nearest thing to what we now mean by phenomenology, the presuppositionless description of experience, was to be found in Descartes and long before him, in the writing of St. Augustine; Hegel used it but not in the present sense. It was Husserl who popularized the word, but this was ten years after the publication of the Principles. In 1890, especially in the "stream of thought," William James gave us what was almost a model of phenomenological thought.

He argued that instead of imposing a set of prior categories on our description of experience, we should begin by observing the experience itself and letting experience dictate the categories (American Psychological Association, 1200 — 17th St. NW, Washington DC., *William James: The Unfinished Business,* 1969). But, this phenomenological view kept all the turmoil within the man. This provides man with no scientific footholds on reality. Phenomenology's abandonment of all hope of finding substantive explanations of the behavior of man need not be man's final answer. He can assume a reality without having to believe that his life is run by it. This brings us to the point where we can selectively agree and disagree with phenomenology. We can agree that we cannot find the explanation of human behavior neatly wrapped in antecedent events. But, we can disagree with phenomenology by declining to accept its implicit assumption that perception is passive (Brendan Maher, *Clinical Psychology and Personality: The Selected Papers of George Kelly*). Also, we must have some mechanism for questioning and confronting our hidden assumptions and categories, because we do have some. If we do not, we run the risk of not being aware of our assumptions which makes man the semantic reactor that he is. Moreover, these hidden assumptions and categories may be false to fact. We apply unconsciously and automatically, perceptions and constructs that might embrace a warped or unsane map of reality (Korzybski, *Science and Sanity*). In short, as we take in the phenomena we ought to know what we are taking it into and automatically practice self-reflexiveness, which enables us to radically revamp our orientation to meet a new reality (Korzybski, *Science and Sanity,* Bois, *The Art of Awareness,* and Johnson, *People in Quandaries*). This does away with self evident truths, with axioms as we learned them in Euclidian geometry, and with snared perceptions. Our set postulates which have grown in a manner similar to the chromosomes and genes must "be examined on an organic" basis (Bois, *The Art of Awareness*). In other words, we develop personal constructs automatically so why not develop them in keeping with the reality processes as we understand them (Kelly, *A Theory of Personality*)? Thus, the place of General Semantics is a container making this process possible; making it possible for us to face unafraid changes in the very structure of our existence (paraphrased from Bois, *The Art of Awareness, Breeds of Men, Explorations in Awareness*).

In current jargon, phenomenology talks of existential experience, a term Tichener used in 1929 in a radically different sense. Locke's word was "idea," Hume's was "impression," and the Germans talked of Vorstellungen — later to be translated back to English as presentations. The fact is that the Aristotelian categories have become so deeply imbedded in our language that we cannot talk about a simple experience without classifying: we are faced with the problem of finding a neutral descriptive language. . . . But will we? (Paraphrased from E. B. McCleod, A.P.A., *Unfinished Papers of William James,* 1969). This is where Korzybski came in with General Semantics in 1933. He developed a non-Aristotelian system in his book, *Science and Sanity.* This equation has been broadened to include the phenomenological approach (see Korzybski, *Manhood of Humanity,* "The Time Binder" and Bois, *The Art of Awareness,* "Epistemological Profile"). Again, I quote McCleod, this time verbatim: "A complete psychology must go beyond phenomenology . . . must be linked with the data of other disciplines." (A.P.A., p. ix.)

Phenomenology is closely akin to the unifying stage of the Epistemological Profile within the General Semantics formulation. This next point is quite crucial and if we miss this, I believe we miss a major difference between phenomenology and the General Semantics formulation. As far as I can tell, General Semantics embraces phenomenology — when we combine first generation methodology and techniques with second generation values and methodology. Incidentally, the discipline is now embarking on a third dimension which is a further development of the part regarding the unifying stage of the Epistemological Profile, i.e., value orientation and the "natures of man," Bois has called this the participating phase. (*Breeds of Men* is the best source.) Dr. Bois is now writing another book, *Organic Philosophy,* which will, hopefully, expand this idea. However, when we apply only the first generation methodology and techniques of General Semantics without Korzybski's concept of time binding, the formulation becomes only a method by which one can practice or implement the phenomenological approach. I say without the concept of time binding, for that concept developed in 1921 in *Manhood of Humanity* was not fully implemented into the literature until Weinberg (*Levels of Knowing and Existence*) and Bois (*The Art of Awareness*) — second generation General Semantics. However, I must mention that phenomenology could be considered an all-embracing philosophy for General Semantics first and second generation methodologies, depending upon one's proclivity to the study of man, how one wants to view phenomena, himself, the world, and most of all what constructs he wants to start with. In short, General Semantics can stand without adopting phenomenology because it already has a "phenomenological" approach. (This sounds like a contradiction in terms but it is not.) Phenomenology, in my judgment, while a sound "process" "concept" "theory" and/or "precept," if we start with it as a "frame," as a "process," is in need of the General Semantics formulation; because, the elements missing in phenomenology, based on my limited knowledge, are "how does one reach" a stage of the phenomenological process? How does one question the hidden assumptions automatically — in other words, how do we build in a self-corrective mechanism? I believe General Semantics offers that opportunity. For emphasis let me reiterate this: when one starts with the General Semantics formulation, he is in the midst of "phenomenology" automatically. When one starts with phenomenology all by itself, he runs the risk of being in the ball park without the bat.

The New Public Administration

We speak of the new Public Administration with a sound

theoretical base. It seems that we may be on to something if we begin to blend these and other theoretical contemporary ideas.

Dr. Bjur's paper on the "New Public Administration" will be used as my point of departure. While I agreed with many of the things he said, I took special exception to the part where he quoted Kierkegaard regarding the use of the either-or dichotomy at the pragmatic decision-making level. It reads as follows:

> "This existential dialectic seems particularly appropriate for the public administrator who knows all too well the world of limited resources where *both* political expediency and ethical or moral justice cannot often simultaneously be served — where an 'either-or' choice is dictated by real world constraints and limited resources . . . when he plunges into existence and confronts the need for ethical choices, he realizes that he cannot become both good and bad at the same time, but he must move *either* in one direction *or* the other."

If this separation is inevitable, then why be "committed to the improvement of the human condition"? Of course, being improved we well might be, but to extend to self renewing and transformation requires a much different approach and special skill. But, whether our objective is improvement and/or transformation when we use the above language, we fall into the old Aristotelian trap of a tight logical system, confusing levels of abstraction and building "static models." If we internalized the "process of abstracting" and held this process as fundamental, our reasoning would be something like this: the valued approach is not only the starter, but, it is also the end product of a decision. Thus, we come to the rather interesting conclusion that the debate concerning the two-valued versus the multi-valued orientation is itself the product of a two-valued orientation. It is not a question of either one or the other; we have to use both. Each is most appropriate at a different level of abstraction. At the non-verbal level, the two-valued orientation is appropriate for arousing our feelings and motivating. At the verbal level of problem solving, symbol using activity, the multi-valued orientation is most valuable. Then, when decision is reached, it is *phrased* in a two-valued fashion so that it can direct non-verbal action, the doing of which is not words. So it is not a matter of simply choosing between one thing or the other — the process is one of vertical abstracting and we move up and down — without interruption until a decision is reached (Weinberg, *Levels of Knowing and Existence*). I believe Dr. Bjur meant this, but phenomenology could not provide this type of fluid analysis. Thus, another difference between phenomenology and General Semantics. General Semantics engages a dimension of analysis which prevents us from becoming marooned at any one stage of the process. It keeps us in touch with the real process taking place within our internal system. And the awareness of this process taking place within our internal system. The awareness of this process through the consciousness of "abstracting" leads us to a proper utilization and understanding of the multi-valued and two-valued systems. The process is not horizontal but vertical — thus no real either-or! This is a difference which makes a difference.

Without this process as a basis for our orientation — we separate verbally "phenomenology" from pragmatism; and, thus cannot begin to develop a "new" Public Administration (the terminology "new Public Administration" is misleading because it does not recognize man as a time-binder [Korzybski, *Manhood of Humanity*] nor does it pay proper respect to the concept of multiordinality [Bois, *Explorations in Awareness*]). Will discuss this at a later date along with an "Epistemologic Framework."

The phrase "epistemologic framework" brings me to the final point in his paper, Dr. Bjur's Subtopic 3 under Topic III calls for a new "epistemologic framework" — which, incidentally, I considered the hallmark of his paper. The General Semantics formulation provides for this in its second generation methodology and value orientation within the framework of the Epistemological Profile, which will be the subject of another position paper. "The Epistemological Profile" can be found in Bachelard's *Philosophy of No,* and Bois' *The Art of Awareness, Breeds of Men, Explorations in Awareness,* and *Communication as Creative Experience.*

Phenomenology and General Semantics could be considered separate theoretical frames — but, the wiser approach is to consider them as the complementarity described by Oppenheimer, the new way of thinking mentioned by Einstein, the transactional psychology of Ames, and the meta-linguistics of Benjamin Whorf — having a place within the multiordinal framework. The parenthetical statements above point the way to the postulating stage of the epistemological profile, to soaring above contradiction and conflict, where we play with symbolic constructs in easy detachment and search for the proper structural construct — one that matches our silent world (Bois, *Explorations in Awareness*). As a beginning, what about "Phenomenology — General Semantics," instead of "Phenomenology and General Semantics"? This way we connect the two. However, and I say this with all humility, the best way would be to look at both from a multi-ordinal standpoint. That is, start with phenomenology as a doctrine, move to the next level and consider General Semantics the theory encompassing the doctrine, move to the third level and consider them a system encompassing phenomenology — General Semantics, out of this we should try for an umbrella construct. This way we reach a new level of understanding. It could be done the other way around — i.e., start with General Semantics as the doctrine — but this would be less effective. (Bois, *Explorations in Awareness,* "Statements, Theory, and Systems.") The beauty of what is being said here is, we have taken a concept (multi-ordinality) from within the General Semantics formulation in order to analyze, in a detached manner, a situation involving General Semantics. Many of the concepts within the General Semantics formulation can stand alone for a certain kind of activity, but they are more powerful when we just regard them as an element within the total General Semantics framework. The epistemological profile, for example, enables us to classify the other concepts and methodology of the formulation in terms of where they should fit, what level of analysis they can provide, and what the limitations are. I will be more specific in the next position paper.

This future paper will treat several of the major ideas more in depth and relate more directly to Public Administration.

CHAPTER II

A BASIC STATEMENT

Position Paper Number Two

The "New" Public Administration

Some Theoretical Considerations

In Position Paper #1, I talked about phenomenology and General Semantics in a premeditated manner; but, in the future will only allude to phenomenology as I see it relating to General Semantics in my attempt to apply the latter to Public Administration. Likewise, I will refer to other theories, doctrines or constructs — and include them where I think appropriate as I talk about the General Semantics formulation. A few come to mind as I write this — specifically, symbolic interactionism, naturalism, and personal construct theory. It is, in my judgment, a mark of intellectual snobbism which is founded in ignorance to treat these and other concepts as separate containers; and, build them without leaving the way open to relationships with other concepts and elements which may be associated. As I review the literature and defining features of the various concepts I find the authors straining to find a difference which totally separates one concept from another. This attempt taxes the reactive system of those seeking an understanding. For example, Herbert Blumer in his book, *Symbolic Interactionism: Perspective and Method,* wrote:

"The term 'symbolic interactionism' has come to be used

> as a label for a relatively distinctive approach to the study of human group life and human conduct . . . symbolic interactionism in the last analysis is based on these premises: The first . . . is that human beings act toward things on the basis of the meaning that the things have for them. . . . The second is that the meaning . . . is derived . . . from the social interaction. . . . The third premise . . . those meanings are modified through an interpretive process."

We see here shades of phenomenology (see my first Position Paper), General Semantics, naturalism, and ontological acceleration (personal construct theory, Kelly). The crowning point was when he made this statement:

> "This symbolic interactionism sees meaning as social products, creations that are formed in and through the defining activities of people as they interact. This point of view gives symbolic interactionism a very distinctive position, with profound implications. . . ." (Ibid.)

He turned inward to dissect his conceptual scheme thereby creating needless boundaries which limited his study and locked himself into a system which prompted this statement:

> "There has been no clear formulation of the position of symbolic interactionism, and above all, a reasoned statement of the methodological position of this approach is lacking. This essay is an effort to develop such a statement." (Ibid.)

In my judgment, an attempt to develop methodology and a higher level of symbolic interaction would be the distinctive feature not a turning inward to dissect a premise which is related to many other premises that utilize different terms for talking about similar objectives. This confusion heightens anxiety and impels a splitting of unnecessary hairs. In other words, it is not a difference which makes a difference; and, does not provide us with tools for developing powerful conceptual schemes that unlock a system and hoist us to a level enabling us to develop broad methodology. We must accept the fact that phenomenology is also making a similar statement (see my first Position Paper); also, that naturalism, where it states:

> "Naturalism, as the very term implies, is the philosophical view that strives to remain true to the nature of the phenomenon under study or scrutiny."

is making a similar statement (David Matza, *Becoming Deviant,* "Natural Deviation," p. 5). And that personal construct theory, where it states:

> "Construct theory, or better, personal construct theory — a term which implies that a construct is as much a personal undertaking as it is a disembodied scheme for putting nature in its place — suggests that human behavior is to be understood in a context of relevance."

is also saying a similar thing (Brendan Maher, *Clinical Psychiatry and Personality*: *Selected Papers of George Kelly,* "Ontological Acceleration," pp. 13-14). And General Semantics, when it states that man is a "semantic reactor," (Bois, *The Art of Awareness,* "The Place and Scope of General Semantics," p. 21) is saying a similar thing. In broad terms our distinctive features should be sought through our theoretical inventions that tell us what to expect and our instrumental inventions that enable us to observe outcomes and, if there is correspondence between the theoretical invention and results of the instrumental invention we call that discovery. Otherwise, we assume that natural events go around introducing themselves by name and whispering theoretical revelations into deserving ears (Maher, *Op. Cit.,* "A Mathematical Approach to Psychology," pp. 94-95). The distinguishing features would not be the "nit-picking" between what it is and what it is not, but the power and richness of the total formulation and how it builds more powerful concepts by hoisting itself above the present level in order to establish a more meaningful frame of reference. This may prevent us from being marooned at the stage of looking for distinctive features that are only symbolically different; a stage that is usually an excuse for not moving to the how-to dimension; a stage where we continue to call something "pure theory" which remains abstract and useless.

This is not to suggest that differences do not exist, but the differences at this higher level of abstraction are mostly differences in "phraseology" and are only important when one phrase clarifies, broadens our frame of reference and impels us to take a semantic jump to another level enabling us to become more aware of the total process, as the concept of time-binding does in General Semantics (Alfred Korzybski, *Manhood of Humanity*). And, even in the case of time-binding, which may be considered a higher concept than primary elements within naturalism, phenomenology, personal construct theory, and symbolic interactionism — we can equate for practical purposes. By doing this, we may move from lower to higher and from higher to lower levels of abstraction in an automatic fashion, within each distinct theory.

I have taken particular pains to talk about theoretical assumptions and other seemingly irrelevant points in order to make a point I consider significant; all the time leaving some things misty, hazy and unexplained. The mistiness, however, will be taken care of at the appropriate time, as I proceed with this paper and develop other position papers — (this is the second in a series of five or six). The point I consider significant has to do with clarifying my position relative to other theories and formulations. I want the reader to know that while I'll be using General Semantics, I am fully aware that General Semantics does not cover all and that at certain junctures other theories or formulations may even cover a segment better; but, most of all be aware that I am "non-elementalistic" in my approach; that is, I see formulations, theories, doctrines, constructs as being related, but most of the time occupying different positions in the abstractive process or having their own abstractive processes, thus making them associates (Korzybski, *Science and Sanity,* "Linguistic Revision," p. 94; and Bois — in a conversation Wednesday, December 24, 1969 at his home). This theoretical departure, paves the way for an entry into the "New Public Administration."

The Phrase "New Public Administration"

I stated in my first position paper that the term new Public Administration did not properly represent man as time-binder. I meant by this that we should not separate, artificially, by setting up categories that may not exist; because, our categories determine the way we look at things and thus, our actions in relation to those things. Consequently, in this case, it may mean that we are looking at this concept, "new" Public Administration, as if it were separate from the old. It may not enable us to see the relationship of what is going on now, to what has taken place. It is most necessary that we be able to recognize the field in its totality. If we do not do this, we run the risk of trying to visualize a system that is totally new, when we may be only talking about more powerful concepts that are products of earlier concepts, obtained through multi-ordinal hoisting. In addition, the relationship should be maintained for two reasons: (1) to show the development of a theoretical base which in itself justifies, to some extent, the validity of a discipline; and (2) for analytical reasons which will speak to future growth. (The concept of time-binding means much more than this. This restricted usage was done merely to introduce the term and clarify a point. More will be said on this later.)

An example relating to time-binding, in mind at the moment, is the concept of non-additivity (Korzybski, *Science and Sanity*) or the structural more (Bois, *The Art of Awareness*) meaning essentially what the "span of attention" or its administrative counterpart — "span of control" meant to V. A. Graicunas viz., the "addition" of a sixth assistant by a supervisor may add 20% to his human resources, but adds approximately

100% to the complexity of his task of coordinating (taken from *Papers on the Science of Administration*). In 1937, the Institute of Public Administration, Columbia University, New York, reprinted materials titled *Papers on the Science of Administration* by Luther Gulich and L. Urwick, introducing this concept. At one time the papers were fundamental to the study of Public Administration. Today they are not. Does that mean that we have abandoned the concepts? Not necessarily. Alfred Korzybski based his notion of non-additivity on this concept: He said,

> "I have found empirically that this is invariably useful for the elimination of the individual's inability to handle personal life situations adequately. . . . At the root of the problem lies the significant fundamental difference in the rate of growth between arithmetical progression and geometrical progression."

The contention is that difficulties accumulate in geometrical ratio. If in personal life we undertake too many responsibilities, interests, involvements, the complexities grow beyond our capacity resulting in disorganization and maladjustments. A single painful event in childhood or later in life distorts attitudes. A childless couple adds a baby to the family and the complications grow. The individual represents heredity plus environment — is this simply plus one addition or are we talking about a more complex factor? And so on. The point is things are non-additive. More than that, when one thing is added there is a new dimension — "structural more" — once described as the "span of control," then non-additive, and now the structural more. The latter construct allow us to take an expanded look at similar phenomena with a more powerful "lens." The point: the non-additive and structural more concepts do not abandon "span of control" but by looking at it from another point of view (multiordinality) we come up with a hoisted concept with an added dimension. Korzybski said in *Science and Sanity,* p. 265, "If facts cannot be covered by given linguistic forms . . . new methods are invented to cover . . . facts in nature."

And Bois, in *The Art of Awareness*:

> "Our formulation of the structural more applies to a variety of situations in which an increase or decrease of a certain element beyond or below a critical point changes the whole picture . . ."

The feature which makes the phrase structural more superior to the "span of control" and "non-additive" concepts is that it not only speaks to numbers geometric in nature but it calls attention to a different and more complex pattern.

As Bois says in the *Art of Awareness,* pp. 104-106:

> "They are not differences in degree, as the additive more implies, they are differences in kind. . . . For the structural more — or the structural less. There is a corresponding change in our semantic reaction patterns."

It tells us that elements have been combined, integrated, arranged, and structurally different than before; we take a semantic jump into a world of different dimensions (Bois, *Explorations in Awareness,* "Introducing the Structural More," pp. 164-165). Bois adds:

> "The whole of man, is not simply the psychophysical nature that he has in common with other members. . . . It is the individual, highly differentiated semantic reactor that each of us is unique in his past, his environment, his anticipated future, and in his thoughts, feelings, values, and bodily habits." (*The Art of Awareness,* "Multidimensionality and Complexification," p. 104.)

The concept moves us to a more sophisticated understanding, but it does not tell us how to deal with the complexity of the human situations produced by the phenomenon. Thus, back to my point — we must continue to develop superior concepts that not only speak to a more comprehensive analysis but will add the dimension of human management. The concept of time-binding may enable us to produce this new dimension. As Korzybski said,

> "This neglect to differentiate between laws of growth of arithmetical and geometrical progressions . . . was partially responsible for most historical spasms of civilization such as wars and revolutions and accounts for many disasters in private lives." (*Manhood of Humanity,* Appendix IV, "Efficiency for Human Adjustment," p. 70.)

So, we move from "span of control" (geometric increases) to non-additivity (cross relationships) to structural more (synthesis, structure and new dimensions — semantic jumps and new levels requiring a totally new orientation).

We build upon the old in a time-binding fashion which speaks to renewal, change, transformation and emergence rather than new without antecedents (Bois, Communication as Creative Experience, p. 8). Likewise, I am sure, as time passes and as we work from the structural more, a powerful construct will eventually emerge. Thus, no old, no new, because this speaks to stopping and starting, a static instead of a fluid equation giving rise to mutation through a process.

Special efforts were made here, not just to quibble over what we call or label what we do; but, to indicate that our labels have their roots in conceptual activity and determine, to some extent, how we navigate, proceed, and manage ourselves. Another byproduct is, it gives an example of how conceptual activity helps to form a base for a discipline, in this case Public Administration.

My third paper will move more forcefully into the areas of Public Administration and General Semantics.

Reflections, Corrections, Criticisms, and Notes on First Position Paper

(1) Dr. Bois disagreed with the placing of phenomenology in toto on the unifying stage of the Epistemological Profile. He

believes that by differentiating between stages in phenomenology and building phenomenology in a multiordinal fashion, i.e., developing a method to study the phenomenology of the phenomenological process, we may begin to equate the two. The reasoning: phenomenology may be confused with the sensing stage, which is Stage I of the Epistemological Profile, unless we make distinctions and build phenomenology in stages. If, for example, we take in phenomena and react with whatever we feel, we could be at any stage at any given time. And, our reactions may be at the primitive level which does not take into consideration that we can manage ourselves and react differently if we so choose; or, that we should in order to manage the situation better. (More of a discussion will take place regarding this when I discuss the Epistemological Profile. Conversation with Dr. Bois on Wednesday, December 24, 1969.)

(2) The phrase "assumptions false to fact" — when we say "false to fact" it assumes a reality out there. It would be better to say assumptions inadequate to present experience. (Page 4, Position Paper # 1, Chapter # 1).

CHAPTER III

THIS IS WHERE I STAND NOW

Position Paper Number Three

The "New" Public Administration

I said in Position Paper #2 that I would move more forcefully into areas of Public Administration and General Semantics in my third position paper. Thus, I begin. I am a General Semanticist, a third generation, hopefully. One of the tasks, as I see it, is to define the direction of Public Administration and move from there into what we need in order to get where we would like to go. Before, however, we reach that point we need to explore some facades of Public Administration. We have a tendency, in my judgment, in teaching to separate the theoretical from the practical, to differentiate between training the researcher, theoretician, teacher, and the pragmatist or practitioner. I am inclined to believe that these categories provide us with a direction that is inadequate to present experience. I do not believe that we can separate our discipline and teaching into such fine categories. I believe we must teach Public Administration, in terms of a direction dedicated and committed to a frame of reference in keeping with that direction and that alone must be the distinguishing factor. Herbert Blumer in *Symbolic Interactionism,* "Perspective and Method," p. 165, said:

"The milling and halting condition of our own sciences

does not come directly from the inadequacy of our techniques . . . but from the inadequacy of our point of view. . . . Like other sciences . . . we await a conceptual framework which will orientate our activities into productive channels."

In other words, our basic view of the world will determine the validity of our concepts and the soundness of our discipline no matter what end product we define. Our theoretical assumptions will become an empirical science for our natural world. Breaking the discipline up into parts may not enable us to build this basic view — especially if we decide our means must match the ends. It is necessary for example, for a practitioner to devote serious study to finding and defining a theoretical framework in keeping with the most progressive thinking in the social sciences.

I am quite prepared, at this time in my life, to enunciate such a position and commit myself to a theoretical frame of reference and a basic view of the world which I think will move us to operate metaphysically and empirically; i.e., metaphysical and empirical being used as co-joined concepts (as map and territory) and as a means for separate analysis of two different types of phenomena in the abstracting process as far as conceptual activity is concerned. I stand, however, just as ready to correct or renounce this basic position in light of new facts and experiences. *This, then, is where I stand Now!*

I have had the opinion for some time that we, in Public Administration and other social sciences, are afraid to put forth a forceful position. Afraid of being wrong; afraid of being involved; afraid of values; afraid of being "political," and afraid of being committed.

"To be involved is to realize that whatever happens, happens to oneself too, that whatever is done, he, too, has had a part in doing it. That is involvement. . . . But, involvement is not enough to generate effective strategy. . . . The human venture is not an exercise in prime receptivity nor

> is understanding developed out of sensory experience alone. So he commits himself to a human course of action. Without doing so he can never know what relevance his own construction of life has to the lives that others live . . . so in undertaking commitment strategy . . . requires one to take deep personal risks." (Brendan Maher, *Clinical Psychology and Personality: Papers of George Kelly,* "The Strategy of Psychological Research," pp. 129-130.)

There is no rigid distinction between life and history, they are interwoven. That is one major reason why the social scientist-Public Administrator must be a political man. (Paraphrased, Domhoff and Ballard, *C. Wright Mills and the Power Elite,* "Comment on Criticism," p. 242.)

Furthermore, it is a moral fault to study things as they are without ever coming to grips with things as they might be. By failing to do this academic Public Administration dooms itself to a static view of society, to the trivial, the obvious, even worse, it seems to justify the present, with all its absurdity, inhumanity, as somehow necessary and right. (Ibid., "The Sociology of C. Wright Mills," p. 13 — paraphrased.)

I believe that Public Administration must not try to keep up with change; but, make the change. We must not only provide knowledge for the leader, but be the leaders. Whatever we are pushing, whether it be phenomenology, General Semantics, symbolic interactionism, personal construct theory, incrementalism; we must make that theoretical frame of reference an aggressive concern and not only improve upon, but transform it into a philosophical concern or position designed to bring about not only an improvement in our basic institutions and systems but change in the very structure of these institutions. (Bois, *Breeds of Men,* Chapter 2, "A Study of Change," p. 22, paraphrased.)

George Kelly said:

> "I seem to have brought myself to a philosophical position . . . when it occurred to me that it was not necessary to . . .

> refute one proposition with another before investigating its alternatives. I was groping toward . . . a philosophical position." (Op. Cit., Maher, "The Autobiography of a Theory," p. 64.)

This requires, if you please, a revamping of our basic orientations and developing of a new kind of faith in mankind. So, inevitably we must be concerned with the how; and, it cannot be separated from the what. Let us then not think in terms of separating these two because a basic understanding of one, if it makes sense, will lead into the other automatically — meaning we do not separate the metaphysical from the empirical except for the purpose of analysis on a high abstract theoretical level — even then we must recognize a process involvement. (Bois, "The Semantic Process of Objective Abstracting," *ETC.*, 1969, p. 349, paraphrased.)

Our journey takes us smack in the middle of a total process. Our tendency to separate one from the other — theory and practice, I believe, represents a fear in going to the "heart" of things. A fear of learning to modify, eliminate or change preconceived suppositions. Consequently, never dealing with the hard issue or posing the hard questions about the nature(s) of man — a concept that will lead to the very nerve center of activity. Instead, we adopt a passive stance, when an "aggressive," calculated, and iconoclastic, self management position is needed. The "passivist" (conservative) by implication says that man cannot remake himself. The risk-taking theoretical-pragmatist says you can remake yourself. I adopt the latter view. The former does not co-join heredity and environment.

Theodosius Dobzhansky in *Mankind Evolving*, "Biology and Culture in Human Evolution," p. 43, said:

> "The biological inheritance of every person consists of genes received from his parents . . . to designate the sum total of the observable characteristics of the organism, Johansen has proposed the term phenotype. The phenotype obviously cannot be inherited; it can only develop as life

goes on . . . all the traits, characters, or features of the phenotype are, of necessity, determined by the genotype and by the sequence of environments with which the genotype interacts. . . . Belief in a sharp dichotomy between hereditary and environmental traits . . . goes hand in hand with a misunderstanding of the roles of social conditions and medicine and education; an hereditary disease is supposedly incurable, a disease contracted by exposure to some noxious environment may perhaps be cured; if the IQ of a child depends on his school's then it cannot be hereditary. The dichotomy of hereditary and environmental traits is, however, untenable: in principle any trait is modifiable by changes in the genes and by manipulation of the environment. All human genotypes respond to some extent to management . . . all character traits are both genotypic and environmental."

We have made two points here: one is, by manipulating the language — co-joining the concepts we develop a different understanding of heredity and environment; and, two, we see that man is not only in charge of his environment through his genetic make up; but, how he thinks, what he thinks about and the direction he takes can be determined through self management. So the fatalistic ideas that man thrives on conflict, and he has to work his problem out through wars can be somewhat refuted and managed with man invented tools — new concepts, symbols and language methodology. This is the one value of General Semantics in being applied to Public Administration endeavors. Methodology points the way to a management of our situation and proper decision-making.

Theodore Longabough in *General Semantics,* "What Type of Life is Man?" pp. 79-80, comments:

"The whole accumulation of words, when organized in an order similar to that of the realities outside their heads, also constituted a body of knowledge of environment and of natural order — a symbolistic copy of the world and of life. They made constant use of words in the processes of knowing, thinking and communicating. This was a turning point in human existence. From then onward men made their adjustments to environment in a new way — not direct (through the senses) as all other animals must do, but indirectly, through the medium of symbolization . . . this copy world in the head.

Their misconceptions were due to their inability to apprehend the symbolistic nature of language and to their acceptance of language as being one with the real world and natural order or, indeed, superior to them; but especially to their unawareness that articulate knowing, thinking, communicating and articulate consciousness all were functions of language.

General Semantics, as set forth in this book, undertakes to demonstrate that knowledge, reason and mind (rationality) are not the primary characteristics of civilized humans that they still are widely supposed to be, but only functions of more elemental structures, mechanisms and processes associated with the objectifying, hoarding and manipulating of perceptual and conceptual abstractions in the brain. They are neither things nor states but dynamic processes, propelled by energy from foods eaten.

What, then, was the distinguishing characteristic of civilized man? It was that he had come to be the symbolizing type of life; the type that had learned the trick of objectifying and hoarding its abstraction as a copy of reality — a substitute for the real world and natural order."

This is where I stand! The question becomes, how do I more intimately relate the above General Semantics position to Public Administration. Before we answer that question, others must be posed and dealt with. From where did we come? Where are we now? Where are we going? And how do we get there?

The assumption then, is that we can know only from where we have come and then where we should be going by first giving some space to what practical men and scholars have thought the field or organization of Public Administration to be.

It has been said that ideology is a hindrance to a sure group of truths, but no less for that, it is also a source of insight. The better we understand organizations, institutions, systems and society in the abstract (metaphysically-empirically), the better we can understand our role and where we fit. We must understand the nature of the milieu of the functionary, images of man, concepts and theories about organization in order to focus and find direction in a world of change and conflict. I propose to do this by dividing my perceptions up into four parts: the Traditionalists, Transitionalists, Behaviorists, and the Institutionalists and then project where I think we ought to be.

The Traditionalists

To understand our history, culture and background, to some extent, as far as our organizational life and its place are concerned, I think it would be wise to begin our chronological discussion with Emile Durkheim, the French sociologist who did most of his scientific work between 1882 and 1912. He was concerned with what he saw as a loss of a sense of community in modern society, a fragmenting, a pulling apart which was due ultimately to the progress of the division of labor (the title of his doctoral dissertation and his first book). Contrary to the individualistic, laissez-faire economic and psychological philosophies of individualism of his time, Durkheim understood that a line of work is not simply something one takes up either as a rational expression of self-interest or as meaningless drifting, inconsequential, adaptation to circumstance. Instead it is a crucial act by which individuals integrate into society and find a definition of society and self. There is a degree of hopefulness in Durkheim's view because he sees satisfaction as a group rather than individual phenomenon, the idea tying in with our present views on man and the cosmos. As Lancelot Law White in *Main Currents,* p. 5, expressed it:

"There is a likelier answer. Homo sapiens may be a social organism uniquely endowed with an organ of understanding, which cannot develop the harmonious, viable, and stable mode of life appropriate to its hereditary constitution and potentialities until that organ has achieved biological maturity by the attainment of a comprehensive balanced understanding of the universe and of its own proper mode of living. This is scarcely a hypothesis. It is good biological sense. A species capable of understanding must possess balanced understanding in order to survive. Otherwise in the excitement of exploiting partial and unbalanced knowledge it will destroy itself."

Work is important, said Durkheim, and its real significance lies in the fact that it locates workers in relation to each other and provides the existential grounding of the social bond that, *latently,* unifies them. Much of Durkheim's perspective is evident in the works of Mayo, Roethlisberger, and Dickson, who analyzed the results of the Hawthorne Studies of management and the worker in the late 1920's and 1930's and the social anthropologist W. Lloyd Warner who carried out the Yankee City Studies in the 30's and of the contemporary industrial sociologist William Foote Whyte. (See for other details F. William Howtown's, *The Functionaries.*)

Max Weber's concern was for the individual. In spite of the difference in emphasis, Durkheim and Weber reached similar conclusions on one key point, it was that the New Society, more and more has a milieu of social and work relationships. But, they disagreed on the point that it was possible to develop corporate self consciousness and save society as a community.

Weber was not alone in his bitter pessimism. Joseph Schuupeter, the economist said, "We have a faceless army of white collar workers."

The chief difference between Durkheim and Weber is that Durkheim emphasized the satisfying social bond and Weber's interest was in the work itself.

The Transitionalists

Mary Parker Follett, an American professor of Public Administration, is remembered as one of the first to reject the rationalism and individualism still taken for granted by most scholars and theoreticians in the 1920's. She insisted that administration should be viewed as a "creative process." She saw the organization as something like an "organism" with its own "life process." The individual experiences his own act as part of a larger collective act which is continually being built up over a period of time. The administrator, once he understands this, will not drive, pull, or push, or "passively administer" but genuinely lead.

Elton Mayo was a social anthropologist who spent most of his career teaching industrial management at Harvard. Like Mary Follett, he found himself out of sympathy with the rationalistic individualism. And, like certain of his colleagues, viz., W. Lloyd Warner and Margaret Mead, he felt and responded to a sense of mission. One of his most important themes was that collaboration could not be left to choice. Looking at societies "close to nature" — preliterate ones, we see that individuals naturally cohere into groups; and, collaboration can be left to choice because the groups are small. In the larger settings, however, it is necessary to plan. In the classic Hawthorne Studies it was concluded that workers were members of a group and considered themselves part of a larger society other than that found within the organization.

Follett and Mayo were pioneer theorists of the organization as a society perspective, and exemplified in their work the bent of the whole vanguard school of the 20's and 30's. There were two schools of thought: one saw coordination as a problem and the other cohesion as a problem. Both took issue with "individualistic rationalism" and proposed in its stead "systemic integral groupism." Neither Mayo nor Follett spelled it out, but from the standpoint of history of organization theory, the postulate is implicit in their scheme.

Bois expresses it this way in *The Art of Awareness* Etc. December, 1969, p. 395:

> "In objective abstraction we do not see the individual person as simply a member of the metaphysical class 'man.' We may see him as an aspect, an element, a constitutive part of a larger unit to which he belongs, be this his family, his nation, or humankind itself. We see him as a fellow participant in a unit to which we belong ourselves, and the welfare or the success of the unit to which both of us belong is much more easily seen as an acceptable concern of yours.
>
> What we have in common is our belongingness to a super-unit, and this vital link supersedes all individual differences. To maintain the super-unit in existence and to make it prosper becomes the purpose of each single constitutive element, which sees in the maintaining and in the prosperity of the super-unit its own survival and success. This was evident during the second World War in England, when social class distinctions, formerly so strong, were practically abolished. The good of all had become the good of every single individual.
>
> To go up in objective abstraction is to train oneself to experience as empirical realities units that are gradually more and more comprehensive, and to subunits as aspects of these larger units. As we broaden our views we bring our feelings to the same comprehensive level, until we learn to live according to the statement of the Latin poet. 'Humanus sum, et nihil humanum a me alienum puto.'"

The Behaviorists

Researchers and theorists are interested in how the individual adapts himself to the organization; how he learns to play his role and eventually how he plays it in fact; how he relates to others, interacts with others, accepts the direction of others or gets others to accept his bidding; how he communicates and receives communication; how he decides what to do (makes decisions) and actually does it (carries out decisions). In short, researchers and theorists who take the individual human act as the strategic datum for understanding the organization contribute a body of work I call the behavioral strand. The following writers exemplify the type: Kurt Lewin, Chester Barnard, Herbert A. Simon, and Chris Argyris.

While these authors concentrated on organizations per se, it is safe to say that they were metaphysical in their approach. Barnard talked about the "strategic factor" as it related to the empirical world of organizations. Simon talked of fact and value metaphysically and Chris Argyris spoke of personality and organization metaphysically. Always striving to connect their concepts with the synthetic or empirical world. If we use relational abstracting to classify this activity, we are well on the way to determining where the behaviorist school fits within the General Semantics scheme — more will be said about this classification when we focus more directly on the General Semantics process. Bois puts it this way, "Relational abstracting gives me the pure theory that never fits *'exactly'* in practice." (Bois, *Explorations in Awareness,* "Finding My Way in the World." p. 137; my emphasis.)

We must, if we are to communicate and develop a discipline, put heavy emphasis on a good solid theoretical framework. And, be sure that that framework contains in its metaphysical structure sufficient relationship to the empirical world. Moreover, that both metaphysical and empirical can be internalized. Socrates' "Know Thyself" will be put in the museum of antiquity, with the logic of Aristotle and the ideas of Plato unless it is translated into action. We must move from knowing what it is to what to do with it.

The Institutionalists

The group of theorists and researchers whose work constitutes what I call the institutionalists' strand, to name a few, are: James Mooney, Alan Reiley, Berle and Means, Peter F. Drucker, Phillip Selznick, Alvin W. Gouldner and Wilbert Moore.

These take the opposite tack from the behaviorists. They see the organization as a conscious organism, see the organization with institutionalized arrangements in a social setting and raise questions concerning change theory and conflict within that social setting. The behaviorists are interested in many of these things also, but ordinarily they think in terms of organizational adjustment of the individual rather than change in the organization itself, and a neglect of relationships with other organizations and how they function socially in a joint enterprise. The institutionalist phase of our development is closely akin to self-reflexiveness abstracting — when I project outside of myself. It is like a feedback operation. The institutionalists are not just aware of their existence as the behaviorists are. They are aware of their awareness and they think about their thinking. It is the process where we observe ourselves in action (see Bois, *Explorations in Awareness,* p. 134, and *The Art of Awareness,* p. 89).

Brief Summary

Barnard and Simon, for example, see the organization primarily as a system of communications. If things go wrong it must be because of a "communications failure"; somehow people have not understood one another. This conception portrays conflicts over the uses and kinds of power as a symptom rather than a root reality: fix the communications system and you solve the problem. Argyris, Whyte, and others of the "human relations" school take a similar tack when they treat "conflict of interest," or even direct challenges to authority, as the result of a technical defect in the way human relations are ordered. The people involved in such conflicts "have problems" and "need empathy training." Or perhaps the formal-informal structure creates "strains" which can be eliminated through redesign.

The behaviorists, in general, set up their analysis in such a way that the authority of management is never called into question. It is treated as a given, a "system parameter." The complaints or rebellious acts of individuals and groups are symptoms of defective management technique, not a demand for justice. Justice simply is not a factor in the behaviorist scheme. The effect is to legitimate authority implicitly by denying that there can be any question of the abuse of power.

Mooney and Reiley see the organization as a legal and moral system of human relationships, and this is true of the institutionalists generally. Management is responsible for achieving a "correlation of social forces," "coherence," and a harmony of interests. There is never any question of "rights"; management has the responsibility to lead and therefore the right to exercise authority. Peter F. Drucker pushes the harmony argument to the point where he all but denies the right of trade unions to exist because they are without function — or they soon would be if management did its job.

Gouldner is not very different. He sees unions as reactive: when the workers go on a wildcat strike it is because of management's ineptness. There is nothing mysterious about leadership: it is just good technique. Management has a function which is societal, not just organizational; regardless of the quality of the individual performance, the function itself is legitimate.

Selznick and Moore are much less confident that "science," or management technology, will save us. But they do see a generalized, society-wide management function; and they wonder about its legitimacy, although in different ways.

Selznick sees management, or leadership in open eyed *realpolitik* perspective: there is a need for leadership and in that sense a leadership-management function. But he is less interested in how management ought to behave than in how it actually does behave. One of its most important functions is to look after its own interests, as a group in relation to other groups.

Moore is less neutral, more helpful as it were. The message between the lines is that management is inevitable because it serves an indispensable function — not just in any one organization but in society as a whole — and so it is in the interest of all of us to help it over its current legitimacy crisis.

Gouldner and Selznick are two of the very theorists and researchers in recent years who have tried to raise and answer significant questions about power in the large organization. This seems odd because there certainly is no lack of a sense of need for better understanding, as one can see in the large body of informed speculation about power by political journalists and others. For example, specialists in the art of "Kremlin watching" or "Sovietology" draw ingenious inferences from relatively flimsy data, indicating a good deal of sophistication about the formation, uses, and effects of power in big organizations — at least in the Soviet Union. In the United States, newspaper columnists (Jack Anderson, Joseph Alsop, James Reston) "watch" the White House and the federal departments, including the Pentagon, all of which are in the public sector, but they pay little attention to the big corporations that constitute the private sector.

Academic social scientists in America pull back from studies of power in big private bureaucracies primarily because it is hard to get financial support, hard to get access to the organizations, and hard to get really good solid data, even after you get access. Some smuggle in a study of power relations while ostensibly doing other research, but then they face the ethical question of violating confidences, stated or implied. Some study power structures and relations from a distance. (C. Wright Mills did this in *The Power Elite,* Ferdinand Lundberg in *The Rich and the Super Rich,* and G. William Domhoff in *Who Rules America.*)

I have sought to explore the development of the field of organization and Public Administration in a chronologically sketchy fashion. Leaving much unsaid about the field; and, in cases where I applied certain concepts that relate to the General Semantics formulation or process — it was done without giving proper General Semantics background. This is so because of my desire to leave a full exploration of General Semantics — the concepts within the formulation, tools and techniques for developing the field — for the end. A decision by design, but, dictated by circumstances and my feelings of what should be. If the reader will please stick with me, the items thrown in at random will be discussed later schematically and will make more sense and I hope will be rewarding and well worth your time.

I intend to show that the field of Public Administration theoretically has developed haphazardly but rather well. The change in focus from transitionalist to behaviorist then to institutionalist which is akin to the transitionalists in terms of philosophy, gives us rather halting position as a time binder. Time binders we have been, but not very effective. Our direction and focus has not been orderly and non-additive (geometrically progression), we have been more related to the additive school (arithmetic). Our jumps have not been dimensional — which would be more tied in with the Epistemological Profile. They, more than anything else, have been multi-ordinal (a step at a time), but, nevertheless a step.

I propose to demonstrate that our next move could and should be a dimensional one. A jump to a new order of things. A new dimension — embracing all in an effective time binding fashion. The order I am speaking of requires a new concept and this concept must match in structure the highest level of the General Semantics formulation as it has been developed to this day — 1970. And, this jump represents a theoretical framework embracing conceptual frameworks in the field of Public Administration. They must be interrelated and linked together in a conceptual pattern, in other words, the concepts must hang together in a system.

For example, we should be using the "law of the situation" concept by Mary Follett and the "strategic factor" concept by Barnard. They are still useful but they do not hang together in a system. I will make an attempt to enable us to hang them together through the utilization of the General Semantics formulation. For the purpose of providing direction, I have projected a new concept — systemic-institutionalist.

The following is taken, for the most part, from Alfred

Korzybski's *Manhood of Humanity,* "Classes of Life," pp. 46-49, along with my own ideas.

To classify phenomena correctly, they must be correctly analyzed and clearly defined. . . . Some say that it is useless and unnecessary to lay so much stress on correct thinking and precise expression; that it has no practical value; for they say that "business" language is good enough to "talk business," or to put "something over on the other fellow." But a little explanation will show that precision is often of the greatest importance.

Humanity is a peculiar class of life which, in some degree, determines its own destinies; therefore, in practical life words and ideas become facts — facts, moreover, which bring about important practical consequences. For instance, many millions of human beings have defined a stroke of lightning as being the "punishment of God" of evil men; other millions have defined it as a "natural, casual, periodical phenomenon"; yet other millions have defined it as an "electric spark." What has been the result of these "non-important" definitions in practical life? In the case of the first definition, when lightning struck a house, the population naturally made no attempt to save the house or anything in it, because to do so would be against the "definition" which proclaims the phenomenon to be a punishment for evil.

Now in the second instance, a stricken building is treated just as any tree overturned by storm; the people save what they can and try to extinguish the fire. In both instances, the behavior of the populace is the same in one respect; if caught in the open by a storm they take refuge under a tree — a means of safety involving maximum danger but the people do not know it.

Now in the third instance, in which the population have a scientifically correct definition of lightning; they provide their houses with lightning rods; and if they are caught by a storm in the open they neither run nor hide under a tree; but when the storm is directly over their heads, they put themselves in a position of minimum exposure by lying flat on the ground until the storm has passed.

another example of sufficient vital importance to be given here, Such examples could be given without end, but there is as it has to do with our conception of the social and economic system, and the state. If our institutions are considered "God-given" — sacred and therefore static — every reformer or advocate of change should be treated as a criminal or "a danger to the existing order." But now, if our institutions are "man-made," imperfect and often foolish, and subject to change all the time steadily and dynamically in obedience to some known or unknown law; then of course all reactionaries would be a "danger to the natural order." The importance of definitions can be seen in all other fields of practical life, definitions create conditions. To know the world in which we live, we have to analyze facts by help of such facts as we know in daily practice.

Some of the greatest and most far-reaching scientific discoveries have been nothing else than a few correct definitions, a few just concepts and a few true propositions. . . . The matter of definition, I have said, is very important. I am not now speaking of nominal definitions, which for convenience merely give names to known objects. I am speaking of such definitions of phenomena as result from correct analysis of the phenomena.

An entire new field may open up; scientific energy may be released in new productive ways. As I see it, this has been the experience of science on the adoption of a new orientation or, what is equivalent, on the adoption of a new conceptual framework. A conspicuous case which may be given in illustration is the origin of modern physics. The work of Galileo is usually chosen, with good reason, as marking the change from the metaphysical preoccupation of the medieval logicians to the scientific endeavors of modern scientists. His work is significant not only for the introduction of experimental technique but also for the development of new concepts which became the basis for the new attack on modern physics. What did this mean? They provided a new perspective: they opened up a new field of endeavor. They raised new problems and suggested new techniques; they sensitized perception to new relations and guided it along new directions; they made experimentation possible, and ultimately they yielded new forms of control. A similar picture, I suppose, is being presented in contemporary physics in the new orientation and conceptual framework surrounding the work in relativity and quantum relations. (This is paraphrased from Herbert Blumer, *Symbolic Interaction: Perspective and Method,* "Science Without Concepts," p. 165.)

Even the purest concept in the social sciences or Public Administration has an ideological dimension, because it is built upon abstractions; and abstractions are made not in a vacuum but from one of a number of possible points of view. The concept is reliable and useful as a tool only if its roots are real and not fictitious. If they embody the ideal and material interests of real people in real situations, in a real world, it follows that any concept is biased both in its source, and in its consequences. A particular way of construing reality if it is to have any human use, inevitably hurts some people's interests and helps others'; it makes out "the truth" to be one thing and not the other; systemic-institutionalist is such a concept.

Systemic Institutionalists

This brings us to where we ought to be in terms of our focus. I have coined a new construct, which makes sense to me. It embraces the new thrust in society and puts Public Administration into a new perspective. I call this new construct "systemic-institutionalist." It means that society in all its complexity must be studied and dealt with habitually by Public Administration. It means that Public Administration must not only study what is, but what might be. It means that Public Administration must not only be concerned about the institutions, but, about the system which embraces the institutions. Moreover, it must be concerned not only with the system but radical and revolutionary systemic changes. So, Public Administration must not just concern itself with institutional change, but systemic social change. It has to move beyond behaviorism within organizations and the change of institutions within the system to thoughts and ideas relating to a new society.

This does not mean that we should not teach, research, and focus on organizational and institutional behavior. But, identify a larger dimension (systemic-institutionalist) which embraces the others. We must accept the fact that the problem must be attacked from different perspectives. But, that a successful attack at a particular level will depend upon the reliability and adequacy of a frame of reference. The larger view will give us extra strength and enable us to identify the significance of our contribution. It gives us a set of values upon which to determine our action. Most of all, it shapes the way we look at things, the decisions we will make, directions we take and the kind of concepts we develop.

We, in Public Administration, for the most part, are functionaries. The crucial question is what kind of functionary we are — the logical (behaviorist-institutionalist) or the sociological (systemic-institutionalist). The former buys the system and strives to work within it. The latter works within it, but questions its assumptions and unrelentingly works to change the system by reform or revolution. (F. William Howton, *Functionaries,* "The Functionary," pp. 14-44.)

This new dimension is of the "structural more" type (see Position Paper #2). Perhaps we ought to say something here about the structural more. The structural more is a fascinating concept. It means, simply, that when we, in our human, or even animal worlds, add a single "fact" to a situation it might have a dimensional — thus structural effect on the situation. Some additions more than others, but always some kind of dimensional and structural effect. The results may be negative or positive or both negative and positive — but, the main thing is they speak to structural and dimensional changes and dictate means and ends.

Take the example of football — one player can make the difference between win and lose in almost every game if he has that kind of talent . . . and most other things being equal. The very structure of the whole is transformed.

Take the example of extra-marital relationships. A man adding a girlfriend to his life along with his wife is not just adding, he is "complicating" his life. (Complicating in the setting does not relate to moralizing or saying what ought to be, but what is and might be.) It is not just addition of a sex partner, but the involvement of a new structure which affects his entire mode of operation. It is a move from additive to non-additive or the span of control and from non-additive to the structural more. In scientific terms, from arithmetic to geometry, from geometry to quantum mechanics. This new structure brings not only good times but added pressures and while these "pressures" and "good times" may not be immobilizing they, certainly, ought to be taken into consideration; because, the very structure of his life has changed and requires a totally new decision-making process. The invisible factors in either situation can be a difference which makes the difference in life style, direction and decision-making. The awareness of the process and awareness of our awareness is the key to a more effective utilizing of radial and tangential energies (this comment is found in *The Phenomenon of Man,* by Teilhard de Chardin, pp. 64-65) implemented through the abstracting process and the Epistemological Profile. (More about these processes in the next position papers.)

This represents not just an added factor, but a jump which requires a new orientation in Public Administration. It represents a rejection of the idea of being value free and following the trends of the time. It projects into the area of leadership and defines a new philosophical commitment. It is a move from being rational vs. irrational to the non-rational process (political and value laden) and then to the position of the creative process.

Today in Public Administration we are split between the behaviorists and the institutionalists concept. We should be at the systemic-institutionalist level. The question remaining is how do we get there? The question then remaining is what new methodologies are desired in light of the new direction? The two questions are similar and can be combined. The new sciences and understanding of man can be applied to Public Administration at this level through the General Semantics formulation. You ask how?

I envision this concept as being close to the postulating stage of the Epistemological Profile — listen to this:

An added difficulty is that breed-4 men are new to their own selves. They have just come out of the larval stage when they fed laboriously in "objective" contact with reality like caterpillars crawling along branches and leaves they can devour; they are just beginning to soar in free flight above the world out of which they came, and enjoy its riches as the butterflies feed on flowers. The management of themselves in this newly discovered world of multiple dimensions is still a bit hesitant and uncertain. They are more explicit on what not to do than on what can be done or should be done to make their new life as rewarding as could be. They have to practice new skills: how to understand their new self; how to stabilize their semantic orientation in a dynamic world of infinite dimensions; how to get along with institutions and power groups that might crush them with good intentions and without any compunction. It is with such a training in self-knowledge and self-management that we are concerned.

They are self actualizers, in the sense that Maslow gives to the term. They are of a culture: they know it and they readily acknowledge that they owe a great deal to it, but they are not locked within the tenets and the values of that culture.

They are committed to a definite philosophy of life possibly too rich to be easily formulated into simple statements that they could accept as adequate. It might have been summed up at times in clichés like, "Love thy neighbor as thyself," or some equivalent saying that has lost its full meaning because of a constant repetition that has become shallow and undiscerning. (Bois, *Breeds of Men,* pp. 104-105.)

And, phenomena obtained by observing the same system with two different types of physical instruments or logical postulates may be mutually exclusive, but this does not bother us any longer. Their relation of mutual exclusion is brought to a higher order of abstraction, and this is called complementarity. Thus the biological-finalist view of the living world ceases to clash with the mechanistic-materialist. Freedom and determinism, good and evil, and all classificatory dichotomies fade away when we observe them from this newly conquered height.

What such an orientation could achieve at all levels of human relations, from the life of the married couple to the forum of the United Nations, we can only surmise. Our philosophy of life, limited by the still-undeveloped sciences of man, has not yet begun to renovate itself as our outlook on the physical world has been doing for the last two generations. One of the purposes of General Semantics is to help function more often and more easily at stage four. It takes time, but it proves to be an exhilarating experience. (Bois, *The Art of Awareness,* pp. 121-122.)

We come then to General Semantics. Alfred Worth White in *Adventures in Ideas,* wrote:

> "I suggest that the development of systematic theology should be accompanied by a critical understanding of the relation of linguistic expression to our deepest and most persistent intuitions." (p. 163.)
>
> "The main sources of evidence respecting this width of human experience are language, social institutions, and action, including thereby the fusion of the three which is language interpreting action and social institutions." (p. 226.)
>
> "It is misleading to study the history of ideas without constant remembrance of the struggle of novel thought with the obtuseness of language." (p. 120.)

The following is paraphrased from *Look Magazine,* pp. 48-50, January 13, 1970.

So, as it turns out, there's a whole vast range not only of emotions but of newly grasped sensations that seems doomed to lie locked up, unwordable in our heads. Our language, in its present shape, just can't handle it; and people are slowly becoming aware of this flaw in their tongue.

It is not that conventional language has become inadequate for communicating fresh concepts merely because of a lack of new words; it's because of the whole way of thinking that it forces us into.

Psychologists say all higher levels of thinking depend on language. But at the same time, the structure of whatever language we use affects the way we see the world — influences, in fact, our attitudes and thought processes themselves. Every major language, says Dr. Mario Pei, started as rough-hewn tools "fit only for material communication, and then proceeded to polish and refine itself to the point of becoming a vehicle for abstract cultural thought."

Obviously, our language has done well in keeping its technological terminology polished up. But just where we need it most today, it lets us down. It's clear that there are important new realms of the mind, of interpersonal involvements and levels of perception that defy its ability to convey or communicate — or even to conceive. The whole business nowadays of people talking about ineffable vibrations they receive from this or that suggests the existence of dimensions of reality beyond the outer limits of our language's vocal range. "A change in language," wrote Benjamin Whorf, "can transform our appreciation of the Cosmos."

At the same time, the growing global nature of the human community is about to place enormous demands upon our capacity for interpersonal communication. "Our new environment compels commitment and participation. We have become irrevocably involved with, and responsible for, each other," says McLuhan. Our future, then, requires more than everyone becoming merely multilingual. What we need is a new basis for communication — a new language and along with it, a newly understood function for language itself. Herein lies the critical factor, a newly understood function for language. Our language forces us to conceive so much of life as an endless, goal-focused struggle, a war. And success, in even the most mild endeavors, is depicted in outright battlefield terminology: We grapple with, strive, clash, cross swords, lock horns, tussle, contend, engage, fight for or take the offensive to achieve a triumph, victory, conquest, a win, a mastery.

We tend, too, in this way to use language not as a means of touching souls with others but as a defense, a barrier, with words deployed as little bricks to wall us in and hold other people off. Language tries to deal with reality by manipulating symbols of reality. It hinges on the mind's ability to link sounds with meanings and thereby transfer those meanings.

We do not need to cling to formal grammar to convey meaning. Speech doesn't have to be linear; it can come out as a compressed overlay of facts and sensations and moods and ideas and images.

The last point I have to express before closing out this position paper is a difficult one, but I'll try. I'll try not only to cover the word but a "feel," an "emotion," a "reaction," if you will. I will be misunderstood because some will conclude that I am only talking about words when I say language is one way we can begin to attack our problems. Language, to a large extent, is the key. Not empty static language; but a language which deals with the world of words, thinking, behavior, our nervous system, and "cultural" dimensions. Language shapes the way we think, act, and feel about things. The more accurate and adequate language, the more apt we are to "find our way." I do not contend that language is the only way, only that it is one way. And talking about words and all of their implications — not grammar — it might be better if we had no grammar — I am talking about "reactions," in this instance, meaning how we feel intellectually, psychologically, and emotionally about things. Being at one with those reactions and conveying through statements made can be a marvelous experience. And I do not mean just with words but a new order and way of expressing.

If there is transfer of meaning, there is language. But this transfer, doesn't have to be in sequential order or in sentence or even in words. Numbers or tones or computer beeps will do it. There are some American Indian tongues in which the verb can include the subject, object and all modifiers so that the entire sentence is a single word. The key element in this is a community of understanding, a willingness to comprehend each other's feelings, a group-consciousness — a quality of "us-ness."

And it is precisely this aspect of speech — already a feature with many young people — that can spread worldwide.

Bois puts it this way and I paraphrase — in essence he says: I (collective I) must make a distinction between accepting what a person says and accepting his existence. I do not have to accept his philosophy, values, logic or directions in order to admit that we both occupy space and exist at the same time. This statement becomes multiordinal. It lifts us from the personalized stage to a stage where we begin to concentrate not on what he says, but what makes him say those things. It is bigger than either person involved in the transaction. Thus, the value of the concept of multi-ordinality (Bois' statement can be found in *Communication as Creative Experience*. I do not at this time have the book handy, consequently I am not giving you a page number. Plus, your own exploration might reveal something I have missed.)

I took you on a longer journey than I wanted to, but I realize an intellectual jump is not the answer. There must be an emotional commitment and involvement to what I am saying. Even before we talk about the how, otherwise, I lose you. Regardless, however, I must talk about how we achieve what I am talking about.

A Public Administration which might and ought to deal with the world at large, especially must have adequate means of designing our future. Organization theory and Public Administration is more than managerial ideology, but it is notoriously prone to being used as managerial ideology. I would like to project the field beyond that to a commitment of values and means for making those values workable.

I am, personally, sick and tired of theories that do not spell out possible ways of internalizing vehicles, methods, techniques, pragmatic and/or empirical constructs for realizing in a personal and meaningful way the values and abstract-metaphysical-philosophical positions we pronounce as desirable. I propose to explore with you a mechanism which will speak to this. And, I repeat, it is not the announcement of some grand theory that we should shout about. That is not the distinguishing feature.

We should shout about the methodology which enables us to reach certain levels of existence. This becomes the distinguishing feature. This separates "the men from the boys." This is the difference between mature creativity and creativity at the rote memory stage. This, if you will, is a difference which makes a difference.

Thus, our focus — General Semantics — will be the next topic relating to the "new" Public Administration. Position Paper #4 will specifically journey here.

THIS IS WHERE I STAND NOW!

COMMENTS

I am impressed with the idea proposed by Dr. Ramos, in the third position paper regarding post phenomenology. However, this becomes linear when we view it as being horizontal. I hope he did not view it that way when he used the concept of the parenthetical man. I prefer to think of it not as post, but a new level of existence which could be termed phenomenology of the phenomenology — thus hoisting to another level to observe the lower level. It does not mean dismissing the old, but adding a dimension which will revamp the very structure of the concept — the structural more, if you will.

For a good look at the phenomenological process and what's happening in the field of phenomenology, please read Professor Ramos' position papers. While I do not agree with his postulate that many of the things I am doing could easily fall under the heading of phenomenology, I am grateful that he has given my work some attention. (School of Public Administration - U.S.C.)

CHAPTER IV

SYSTEMIC - INSTITUTIONALIST ELABORATION AND GENERAL SEMANTICS PROCESS INTRODUCTION

Position Paper Number Four

I. *Introduction*

I said in the last position paper that our proper direction in Public Administration at the present time, could be summed up in the construct, systemic-institutionalist. I conclude that this would not only represent a direction, another phase in Public Administration; but, would be a jump to a new level, a new dimension, a change in the very structure, the way we function, and the mental concepts and models we use. I do not suggest that this is where we stop; but, modern and up-to-date epistemology dictates this to be in keeping with the world as we find it at the present time — meaning that we must see relationships, we must have a space-time orientation, we must be effective time-binders, and we must see our relationship to the world and the universe in terms of oneness — meaning that our minutest decision has world-wide or even universe-wide implications, environmental and genetic implications. In other words, what we do will help to make our world and we can partially determine the direction: we are in charge. This, then, imposes a hard responsibility and an opportunity to not only survive, but to live. Plants survive — man has a right to life and living in the most creative sense. This, then, is not where we stop, but where we begin.

I am mindful as I talk about this that up-to-date modern epistemology is just that. It is where we are now. In short, the systemic-institutionalist construct is of a temporary nature. The law of time-binding, the world of epistemology, and the formative tendencies of the universe (the maturing force behind our changes) continue to move us into new directions. Therefore, our epistemology has to be continuously up-dated. The construct systemic-institutionalist becomes a part of the past or the transition stage; but, all we can do is accept to exist today and hope that our premises or epistemological framework is adequate to allow for continual creative building.

In Public Administration right conceptual making activity is very important. The validity of our concepts will determine our progress. If our assumptions are static, non-fluid, and limited we will be limited and narrow in our approach. We must be sure that our assumptive mechanism will enable us to design realities that may be in keeping with man's natural abstractive process (empirically and metaphysically) and values which are in tune with man as an effective time-binder. The usage of the terms empirical and metaphysical tell us in rough terms what kind of reality we are talking about and it makes us know that what we are talking about is a part of a reactive process. And, for purpose of analysis of levels of reality it becomes fundamental. Let us state it fully, succinctly, and honestly — our assumptions about reality, if we are not careful and aware, can make an "ass" of you and me. We are no longer talking about man's survival that is a plant model, we are talking about man's creative potential that is a human model.

It would be interesting and profitable to continue along this theoretical and philosophical way, but we must get on with developing an epistemological framework in keeping with our postulation.

II. *Systemic-Institutionalist Elaboration*

In Position Paper #3, I talked about the systemic-institutionalist construct. I postulated this. Let us suppose that we are systemic-institutionalist; let us suppose that this is the right direction for us to follow.

I put it within the above "let us suppose" context for two reasons. (1) Let us suppose postulate means that I am not hard, rigid, and inflexible. I stand ready to modify the construct. (2) The second reason is the construct is a reductionist construct — meaning that it is reduced or abstracted from something. That something is modern epistemologic-General Semantics framework, which is in turn tied in with the formative tendency of the world which automatically moves us to a new dimension. But, regardless of that knowledge, we must accept where we are.

If the systemic-institutionalist framework is a good one — meaning that we are concerned with society at large, even the cosmos and what is going on (WIGO) — our concepts, constructs, and attitudes will reflect this.

Our postulate that the systemic-institutionalist construct is in keeping with the formative tendency of the world, the universe, the cosmos, and is our correct direction, at this time, for Public Administration — dictates the raising of the following questions. What kind of value system should we develop? What methodologies, tools, and techniques should we focus on to implement this value system? Where did this value system and these methodologies come from? We answer these questions by focusing on up-to-date or modern Epistemology better known as the General Semantics process.

Let me take the questions in this order: third question first, then first question, then second question.

III. *Emergence of General Semantics: An Historical Perspective*

Let me now put our discussion in some kind of historical perspective. From where did the values and methodologies come?

In 1921 a Polish mathematician by the name of Alfred Korzybski published a book entitled *Manhood of Humanity.*

His feelings were, since he was an engineer, that by applying the principles of engineering to our human problems it might be possible to make more progress in public and human affairs. He was chiefly concerned with the fact that the great disparity between the rapid progress of the natural and technological sciences on the one hand and the slow progress of the metaphysical or the social sciences would sooner or later redistribute the equilibrium of human affairs and results periodically in social cataclysmic insurrections, revolutions, and wars. These are violent readjustments in human affairs and the disparity widens as we pass from generation to generation. They not only occur with increasing violence, but with increasing frequency. It is interesting to note that Korzybski's construct (appears on p. 23 of *Manhood of Humanity,* "A New Concept of Life") which is the additive nature of government and political progress and the non-additive nature of the technological progress found its way into the management literature in 1934 in the works of Walter N. Polakov, engineer and industrial diagnostician in the form of a communication written for TVA which included a summary of Graicunas' work "span of attention" later "span of control" which we studied in *Papers on the Science of Administration,* by Luther Gulick and L. Urwich (see Appendix IV, Some Non-Aristotelian Data on Efficiency for Human Adjustment, pp. 265-277, *Manhood of Humanity,* included in the 1950 edition. There is also reference to this in my Position Paper #2). The major construct, in his work, however, was the theory of time-binding.

In 1933 he published his major work, *Science and Sanity.* In that work he developed a complete Epistemologic framework, which he called General Semantics. He had originally intended to title the book *Time Binding;* but, changed the title practically on the eve of publication. His works were developed entirely independently of "semantics." The original manuscript did not contain the word semantics. He introduced the term General Semantics which means something entirely different from Semantics as we know it. The "semantics" he introduced was a jump from the study of words and symbols, grammar, language and the such, to an empirical natural science of non-elementalistic evaluation taking into account the living individual, his reactions, his neuro-linguistic and neuro-semantic environments. His was not a concentration on the language but the very structure of language. A non-Aristotelian modern epistemological system, if you will, with the structure of language as the dimension for revamping our knowledge and supplying us with the vehicle for changing our very lives. The socio-cultural input, however, which is only implicitly in *Science and Sanity,* is explicit in *Manhood of Humanity.* It adds up to the following:

> "We need not blind ourselves with the old dogma that human nature cannot be changed, for we find that it can be changed. We must begin to realize our potentialities as humans; then we may approach the future with hope." (*Science and Sanity,* Preface to third edition, Oct. 1947, p. xxiii.)

He proposed to accomplish this by relating linguistics structure to the structure of non-verbal levels, in connection with a theory of values combined with extensive techniques for educational guidance and self-guidance. Such a theory requires a modern scientific approach based on physio-mathematic methods. Based also on the capacity to produce higher and higher abstractions which eventually culminate in a general consciousness of abstracting, the very key to further human evolution. The application requires, according to Korzybski, "a systematic codified way of thinking, non-Aristotelian in nature." Thus, the beginning of our modern epistemology with the language dimension known as General Semantics (conversation with Dr. Bois, Wednesday, January 21, 1970 at his home).

My interpretation of the history of General Semantics can be divided into two phases. First and second generation phases — generations in this instance meaning the quality of the contributions not chronological age.

The first generation General Semantics can be roughly classed as those who dealt with the original formulation of Alfred Korzybski without questioning many of the basic assumptions or dealing with the premises in a theoretical sense. They are mainly concerned with application and implementation through the extensional method. This school is composed, for the most part, of: Wendell Johnson, *People in Quandaries;* S. I. Hayakawa, *Language, Thought and Action;* Irving Lee, *Language Habits in Human Affairs;* Katherine Minteer, *Words and What They Do To You;* Kenneth S. Keyes, Jr., *How To Develop Your Thinking Ability;* William V. Haney, *Communication and Organizational Behavior;* Paul Pigors, *Human Relations;* Stuart Chase, *The Tyranny of Words;* Anatol Rapoport, *Operational Philosophy;* and Bess Sondel, *The Humanity of Words.*

There is a group I would not place in either generation. They appear to have taken pieces and dealt with them in depth; or, dealt with the subject from the standpoint of commentaries, criticisms. Some who fall in the former category are: Benjamin Whorf, *Language, Thought, and Reality;* Kenneth Burke, *A Grammar of Motives;* I. A. Richards, *The Meaning of Meaning;* Theodore Longabough, *General Semantics;* Margaret Gorman, *General Semantics and Contemporary Thomism;* Edward Hall, *The Silent Language;* Weller Embler, *Metaphor and Meaning;* and Dan Fabun, *The Dynamics of Change.* Some of these, in a manner of speaking, could be considered links or Transitionalists who were not sufficiently committed or immersed or both to really come to grips with the broader epistemological framework and its implications.

The second generation general semanticists are few. I can only accept two and one with reservations. The one with reservations is Harry Weinberg, *Levels of Knowing and Existence.* Harry Weinberg went back to Korzybski and not only tried to put Korzybski in modern day terminology but to emphasize the fundamental process of abstracting with the value premises Korzybski enunciated in 1921 in *Manhood of Humanity.*

The other person whom I consider a second generation General Semanticist is J. Samuel Bois, *Explorations in Awareness, The Art of Awareness, Communication as Creative Experience,*

Breeds of Men and a manuscript in preparation called *Directions.* He has not only dealt with the fundamental postulates of Korzybski, but has come up with formulations of his own. Bringing about an additional dimension to the Korzybski epistemological framework by including a formulation called the Epistemological Profile developed fully in *Breeds of Men.* Begun in *Explorations,* continued in *The Art of Awareness* and *Communication as Creative Experience.*

His contributions brought about a semantic jump, in thinking regarding General Semantics, of the structural more type. His framework — based on Bachelard's profile in the *Philosophy of No* — has brought about, in addition to the semantic jump, a revamping of many postulates within the Korzybskian Epistemologic framework, without discarding any of the original notions.

The fact is that Bois has been able to include within his frame of reference Korzybski's Epistemological framework — Korzybski automatically is brought into the second generation — which could easily be considered the Bois era, but does not exclude Korzybski. It is merely the structural more and time binding constructs in operation. It probably is a classic example of effective time-binding as explained by Harry Weinberg.

Bois' contributions are best summed up by Robert Wanderer, member of the editorial committee of *Etc.,* and past president of the San Francisco chapter of I.S.G.S. In the December edition of *Etc.,* The Journal of General Semantics honoring Dr. Bois, he wrote:

> "Dr. J. Samuel Bois is clearly, I think, the leading theoretician in General Semantics today, as well as a valuable and exciting explorer of how to apply it. . . . He is neither an orthodox Korzybskian nor merely a popularizer whatever these terms might mean. He builds on Korzybski's foundations and develops insights that I find extremely useful." (*Etc.*: A Review of General Semantics, "J. Samuel Bois: An Appreciation," December, 1970, p. 391.)

Bois is conducting a seminar presently, in the School of

Public Administration at the Civic Center Division, thanks to our Associate Director K. William Leffland and John Parker, Director of Civic Center Campus and, to Bois for giving up the time. The course is a 501 entitled Public Administration Problems: Administrative Skills for a World of Change.

I did not include all in the field of General Semantics — most of the ones listed were landmarks in whatever they tried to do. Most of them can be considered "popularizers" and "appliers."

Briefly, this is how General Semantics Epistemology emerged. Now, what kind of value system does it dictate?

IV. *Time-Binding Construct: A Value System*

I must begin with the proposition that man is a time-binder. We must start with a proper starting point for a science of humanity. The characteristic nature(s) of man have to be defined. The conception of man as a time binder embraces the whole of the natural philosophy, the whole of the natural sociology, natural economics, it is concerned with human engineering. Everything time binding represents that human progress ought and might stand for. A sharp line is drawn between animal and man. Everything space-binding will be classified as animal.

Human beings are characterized by their creative powers, by the power to make the past live in the present and the present for the future by the capacity to bind time. Humanity, in order to live, must produce creatively, and the so-called social sciences must be emancipated from the medieval metaphysics that man is an animal, a certain kind of animal, or that man is a mixture partly biological and partly philosophical, or that man is a combination or union of animal with something supernatural. Both of these models are radically wrong. There are basically three classes of life; plant — chemistry-binding, animal — space-binding, and man — time-binding. These definitions represent not only definitions of different classes, but distinct dimensions. No measure of rule applied to man literally or metaphorically can produce correct action. To treat man as an animal because he has certain assumed propensities is a mistake of a horrible dimension. What we do flows from our basic definition of man. We must have a proper starting point.

The solutions to social problems have mostly been zoological and mythological. The zoological solutions are those which grow out of the false conceptions that human beings are animals and so the social sciences — ethics, law, politics, economics and government — become branches of zoology. They are the acts of managing and controlling animals — according to this zoological philosophy, human wisdom is animal wisdom.

The mythological are those which start with the conception that we have no separate place in nature, that we are a mixture of animal wisdom and supernatural divinity. So, the construct of time-binding, which rejects the above, is fundamental. We must discover the values, inherent in effective time-binding, and allow our constructs to flow from this kind of "fountain."

Our values concerning the "survival of the fittest" will mean excellence in science, art, wisdom and justice — in the sense of the strongest we will realize it is an animal standard — the standard of the beast. This is a space binding value.

Our attitude concerning wealth is that time binding is not merely a civilized life, but a civilizing life. Properly, we will begin to feel that material and spiritual wealth is a natural phenomenon, offspring of the marriage of time and human toil; that wealth or the world at any given moment is almost the wholly invented fruit of time and the labor of the dead. We will teach that each generation is a trustee for the next and the "goodies" should be passed on to everybody; we will teach that the "capitalist" propensity to keep for self and proletarian cornering of the market are both *space binding* and beneath the level of *time binding;* we will know and understand that the common aim cannot be the welfare of family, one state, or one race but the welfare of all mankind. We will commit ourselves to the proposition that there is a value in having values. What makes one value superior to another? The superiority of the value is determined by whether or not it speaks to survival and living.

We begin with a basic assertion that the survival of the human race is important; that tapping man's creative energies is indispensable. The problem then is to determine what things are likely to contribute to survival and the emergence of creative energies.

A basic value within the time-binding construct is holding ideas tentative — questioning whatever values we have committed ourselves to. This is a value to question values. One develops a love which is neither sentimental nor hypocritical. In order to achieve these values, he must have a value of being selfish on a higher level (self actualization) in order that he can be unselfish on another level.

Our value system must be overarching in order to embrace the matters having to do with social concerns. This can be accomplished by having a commitment to have a world wide outlook; a commitment to function at the highest level possible as a human, not human animal; a commitment to stay in touch with the latest thinking in modern epistemology and thinking concerning man; a commitment to develop a philosophy of life that soars beyond the various vehicles we use to accomplish larger objectives, a philosophy of life which commits us to theory that will stand the test of time and have confidence that it is tied in with the proper direction of mankind, an unwavering commitment except in the light of a new understanding; a commitment, if you will, that gives us the courage of our convictions; and, know that specific decisions made within our frame of reference will be in keeping with where the world ought and might be. It will not only be what we stand for, but what we will die for, if not literally, symbolically.

Our understanding is that man can make little more than incidental decisions; but, that those incidental decisions find expression within a broad philosophy — based on survival and man's creative potential — thereby enabling a sociological functionary to have sufficient impact on the broader issues. It is intertwined with a belief that if a functionary functions as a philosopher and with the latest advancement in the ologies, he will have an impact; at the same time realizing that this framework of values makes it possible for the emergence of constructs such as systemic-institutionalist which, then, is only a theory within a larger theory awaiting changes that might be.

Bois sums it up as follows in *The Art of Awareness,* "The World in Which We Live," p. 185:

> "But there is a second tendency, which is a true manifestation of time-binding energy. It is the tendency to keep reexamining a new system of thought in the light of its own development, to keep stirring revolutionary thinking so that it won't jell into tradition. This second characteristic is the one that holds promise for the far-reaching future. If we accept time-binding as the law of human nature, this continuing attempt at self-renewal is the normal expression of human nature in action, of human nature in the characteristic functioning that differentiates it from lower forms of life. Clinging to tradition, whether it is centuries old or of more recent vintage, is the very negation of that distinctive human characteristic. It brings man one step down, to the level of animal life, where generations after generations keep repeating the same patterns of activity. We thus copy animals in our nervous systems as Korzybski so often deplored."

A value which holds all concepts, all constructs, all theories, all postulates and other values as tentative; a value which seeks the highest level possible for operating; the idea that man can make himself, can develop his talent can change things that lead to non survival in the human sense is a substantive value.

The value which holds the above value as tentative is a procedural one. It is at the highest possible level embracing also the methodology for reaching both levels. This is not wishy-washy, it is holding dear the capacity for revamping our basic notions in a self corrective manner.

Finally, it is the art of knowing. There is something about

the act of knowing that makes it necessary for us to see things all at once and together as a whole if we are to arrive at genuine realization or insight. Real peak awareness represents such a radical, instantaneous, global reorganization within the individual. It is the moment of awareness of creative possibilities, and as such, it may be both exhilarating and frightening. It involves a change in the person's conception of himself as well as the form of universe he sees. This change may be particularly striking in terms of his willingness to go along with accepted beliefs and conventions, whether in his discipline, his art, or his society.

In conjunction with the last paragraph, the transitionalist schools of thought in Public Administration — Follette, Barnard, Mayo, etc. were on to something. Our energies, partially in terms of time-binding efforts in Public Administration, could have been on developing theories relative to societal matters as well as behavioral sciences. Understand me now, the behavioral sciences should have been given attention and should be now. But, not in lieu of the larger context. This would have meant a continuation of the other dimensional findings of Mayo, Rothlisberger, Dickson and Follette. They talked about society as a whole. We chopped off that dimension of their involvement; by doing so, we "marooned" our focus on organizational behavior. A development of their additional dimension could have fallen in the category of effective time-binding. This, then, would dictate the kind of education we would have provided; the kind of people we produced, and finally, the way we identified problems.

Before I direct my attention to the *how* of functioning at the systemic-institutionalist level or modern epistemological stage, let me direct your attention to the exploring of a myth and a definition of General Semantics.

V. *Exploring a Myth: Toward an Explanation of General Semantics Epistemology*

Dr. Ramos said in his Position Paper #2, "I have suggested

that phenomenology has a great interest for the social scientist . . . nevertheless, the social scientist *would* be diverting himself from his specific task if he tried to meet the requirements of an orthodox phenomenologist." Whew! (take a pause) I thought it would never be said, now I can breathe with some ease. I no longer feel it necessary to tread lightly — if you missed the above quote, you missed the crux of his paper. We, at that point, joined the worlds of action, change, relativity and quantum.

In order to understand, in specific terms, where we are regarding phenomenology and General Semantics, we must explore a myth. We must realize that phenomenology was written when people thought of things and the world as containing still facts. The world is thought of now as an action world, pluralistics though we are (which is a good concept) the phenomenologists say we relate to things and categories that exist out there. If this were so, we would not have color blind people. Gray is gray because we make it so. We cannot assume that things exist independently of the observer (see Whorf, *Language, Thought, and Reality,* and Weinberg, *Levels of Knowing and Existence,* and Bois, *The Art of Awareness*). Post theory of phenomenology must address itself to the revamping of the original premises. The one premise that phenomenology, as I know it, does not question is the common sense notions of reality. The main idea in the common sense notions is that things are there to be seen. General Semantics assumes that things do not reveal themselves to us and we do the categorizing. You say this is reductionism and it is better to eliminate reductionism. I say you are correct, but that we cannot help but reduce and categorize. Our major job is to categorize properly and be sure our reductions are considered abstractions and realize they do not cover all; thus the concept of non-allness in General Semantics. Karl Marx reduced epistemology to an economic system, Freud applied it to psychology. The major danger is saying that the theory or proposition represents all. This applies to phenomenology and all of the -ologies. The major task is to raise sights to the level of epistemology. I cannot say I am going beyond phenomenology when I accept the original phenomenological basic premises. When I move to the world of action, change, and dynamics I move away from phenomenology. What we are talking about at that point is a modern epistemology; phenomenology is a theory and epistemology is a theory of theories. The formative tendency of the world makes it necessary for all of us to develop a world view based on space-time. This world view becomes a basic philosophy within the realm of episteme and it is subject to change as we develop beyond the present epistemology. Take General Semantics for example, it questions the assumption not only of the basic theories but the assumption hidden in the language of the basic theories. General Semantics is merely a name that has been given to epistemology to accentuate the meaning of the to-me-ness and enable us to raise questions that we have not raised before about our postulates and the structure of our language. General Semantics, itself, then can be considered up-to-date modern epistemology with the understanding that we are working within an overarching conceptual scheme which embraces epistemology of different times and different dates. They could be outlined as follows: postulates (logical), theories (epistemology 1840), system of language (modern epistemology) — language being a postulative system (modern epistemology) which gives a new projection to epistemology.

The second myth I would like to explore is one which assumes that a great number of things which are done in the field of Public Administration can fall under the heading of phenomenology. The assumptions which say that man approaches "reality" "fact" "things" with no preconceived ideas provides us with a flimsy foundation. It would be tragic to call this a postulate because postulates are tentative theories. It is a good attitude and it can only be considered an attitude until the assumptions are revamped in light of present changes that are of the 20th century. Man knows that at the present time, we have preconceived ideas and those preconceived ideas are a part of what we think is real. If we stick to this phenomenological false foundation everything we build from then on contains falsities, to some extent. However, if we consider it an attitude, we do not attempt to build a foundation based on it; we only say that to have an attitude of approaching a situation in a non-preconceived way is a good attitude. And as long as we consider it an attitude and not a postulate we are in good shape. A postulate precedes a logical system. This is where we make a distinction between phenomenology and General Semantics.

Phenomenology can be considered a thought process which represents the world of things and facts. General Semantics on the other hand, can be considered epistemology which gave an added dimension to cultural anthropological thinking, feelings, reactions, language and the study of language meaning that we did not only question the postulates themselves but, assumptions built into the structure of language also. In short, then, General Semantics can be considered modern Epistemology.

Alfred Korzybski had trouble when he wrote his book *Science and Sanity,* in finding a name for his epistemological framework because it added the dimension of language.

Another major difference between phenomenology and General Semantics (modern epistemology) is the eradication of the is of identity. We no longer say a thing is — the moment we do, we speak of sameness and allness, we are in a language trap which creates an objective world.

Now let us face it! There are things out there. Listen carefully now because I am not going to say what you think I am going to say.

When we view the empirical world with our abstracting mechanism, for all practical purposes, we do see things *we call* a tree, a chair, poverty and the emphasis is on 'we call' which is underlined. We defined it, and labeled it. It is only a thing because we said it was. When we say that things exist out there without putting ourselves in the picture, we deny that the label, the word is only a symbol of the thing. A thing did not name itself, we did. The thing contains many more factors or elements than the symbol, word, or label. If then it does exist, why all the fuss? The fuss comes from the fact that when we empirically look at an object we can feel, see, or think we can feel or see, we want to be aware of the process taking place and we can only be aware of the process taking place by making sure that our total mechanism is responding properly to the things we have labeled as things. Otherwise, we reach the conclusion that we have a fact world and a tree would have been a tree without man using his symbol making activity to make it so. Things are what we say they are.

We must adopt the following attitude. Let us suppose that this is so and so. This sounds like splitting so many hairs, in some instances it may be, but it can be a difference that makes a difference. A good example of this is an exchange of correspondence between Dr. J. Samuel Bois and the American Association of University Women. They wanted Dr. Bois to participate in a conference labeled the "Peace Bomb." His answer in part was, "I see it as a war in reverse. It is aping the war mongers to combat war mongering. It is to establish peace by the methods of the war establishment. It is about time to learn our lesson and give up mental constructs of the war-peace-aggression-no-aggression variety." (Letter to Mary A. Seelye, A.A.U.W., dated Nov. 17, 1969.) Are we, here, talking about so many words? No, we are talking about models that determine the way we think and act; and about different means for reaching desirable ends. More than that, whether or not our means and ends construct can bring about lasting change in our long range direction.

The above has far reaching implications. It indicates man has control of his environment, he makes his reality. If he makes it, then he can do something about it if it is not in keeping with what he thinks ought and might be. This becomes a hopeful sign. This tentative and non-identification is important as an attitude of mind. We don't want to go overboard about this, but we want to make sure that we develop, as one student in my class said, "a systemic awareness" of these processes in order that man cannot just merely survive as plants do and take things for granted that they are what they are —

but give him faith in his potential and hope for his future.

Let me close this section by trying to give you a more succinct definition of General Semantics. We must not confuse General Semantics with semantics. The Korzybskian system goes further and the Bois system goes even further. When these two are combined, I come up with something like this: When its implications are worked out, it will be as far removed from semantics as semantics is from logic, and as logic is from grammar. Grammar deals with word-to-word relations. It teaches how to put words together into a sentence. It is not interested in how sentences are related to each other or how they are related to facts. Logic goes further. To a logician, sentences are assertions, and he is interested in relations between assertions (if this is true, then that is true). But for the logician words need not have any meaning except as defined by other words, and the assertions need not have any relation to the world of fact. The semanticist goes further than the logician. To him words and assertions have meaning only if they are related operationally to referents. The semanticist defines not only validity (as the logician does) but also the truth. The General Semanticist goes the furthest. He deals not only with words, assertions, and their referents in nature, but also with their effects on human behavior. For a General Semanticist, communication is not merely words in proper order, properly inflected or assertions in proper relation to referents. (Special Mimeographed Paper — 1967, Williams.)

It is up-to-date epistemology. It is the science of our mental activities. It deals with how we observe with our senses, how we introspect, how we think, how we doubt, how we communicate our own views, how we solve problems, how we invent and how we create. It is a science of the *how* not just the what. It deals with methods and skills. General Semantics is an attempt to organize in a well balanced system, the cumulative findings of man and to develop this system into procedures for self management. The wealth of information and findings are there; our job is to sort out the valid and the useful and devise methods of application that are practical, easily learned and effective (Bois, *The Art of Awareness,* pp. 12-15).

In order to be on the safe side, I prefer to think of phenomenology and General Semantics as alternatives rather than try to refute one in order to project another. That is considered constructive alternativism, which simply means that we do not have to refute one theoretical system in order to project another . . . so we provide alternatives for ourselves and others.

This paper throughout deals with partial truths only — nothing that it contains is intended to be wholly true. The theoretical statements propounded are no more than partially accurate constructions of events which, in turn, are no more than partially perceived. What I propose, hopefully, will be eventually overthrown and replaced by something with more truth.

One of the troubles with good theories in the various fields of social science is the claim to infallibility that is so often built into their structure. We are caught up in the assumptions and structure of the very language upon which we depend for communication. All the theories have weaknesses. They are at best abstractions belonging to a larger epistemological framework — quantum in nature, they take bits and pieces — structure and dimensions that defy complete construction (Maher, *Clinical Psychology and Personality,* pp. 66-68). So, there is room for all. All we ask is that man should not order his life in terms of many special and inflexible convictions about temporary matters which make him the victim of circumstances. The man whose convictions encompass a broad perspective and are cast in terms of principles rather than rules has a much better chance of discovering alternatives. These are the earmarks of men who seek a broader understanding of what they are about. (Kelly, *A Theory of Personality,* pp. 40-42.)

General Semantics, with its two generational aspects, has its place within the broader formative tendency (the world forming itself unnoticed). It is a language dimension of the epistemological framework which makes it more the modern epistemology since it embraces a system of languages, culture, theories, doctrines, postulates — all coming under the heading of WIGO (what is going on) giving rise to the formative tendency. So there is room for both of these processes if we subscribe to the concept of constructive alternativism. It is not one or the other, but how one may develop a personal construct which enables him to move and manage. Where each fits will depend to some extent on the way one defines his world.

VI. *Summary and Projection*

I have taken you through several phases. The systemic-institutionalist construct; the emergence of General Semantics epistemology; time-binding construct as a value system; and, explored the myth surrounding General Semantics epistemology.

The elaboration of the construct indicating where we ought and might be going, tied in with the latest developments in up-to-date epistemology. At that point I explored General Semantics as a possible theoretical source for application; finding a suitable relationship led to a discussion of values, then an explanation of the General Semantics epistemology which embraces those values and supplies methodology for implementation organi-mistically.

The value or philosophy which enables us to function at different levels without becoming marooned at any one level beneath the highest level that we subscribe and enables us to function effectively at all levels, has to be translated into action. So, we begin with the "real" *how* to dimension, through the utilization of the G. S. Epistemological Process. In terms of procedures, we move immediately from the construct of time-binding — which I have talked about as the first step in our *HOW* process — to that of the abstracting process, then to the Epistemological Profile, etc. The last Position Paper #5 will proposition as follows: that by relating and internalizing these constructs, along with their processes, it is possible to be an effective time-binder and deal with our world in a saner manner.

CHAPTER V

THE AUTOBIOGRAPHY OF A CONSTRUCT

I Begin

I had thought, at first, that I would end this five paper series by giving you a glossary of constructs within the General Semantics Epistemological process. Ask you to memorize them and eventually strive to internalize them and make them your own. As I thought more about it, however, I decided that this was inadequate. Then, I hit upon the idea of sharing with you some of my personal experiences with the General Semantics Epistemological process. I know, also, too well, that this is woefully inadequate. The only adequate procedure would be to continue the process with you in constant transaction; but, since this cannot be done, at this time, the latter way appears to be the best. So, I will begin.

Since the capstone will be a New York unifying experience, I have decided to call this paper the "Autobiography of a Construct." It goes beyond that, but I believe it is a satisfactory focus.

My Journey With the General Semantics Epistemological Process

My Background and History

Before becoming involved, immersed, "reacting and transacting," somewhat, with General Semantics Epistemology, I was intellectually committed. And, I only became "reactively" and transactionally, committed, when I began to deal with General Semantics through Dr. Bois and his latest findings and developments in the field. I knew there was something there. I had been searching since 1952, on and off, and had not found that certain something that was akin to a "love affair." Finally, I began to relate to it in the latter fashion. The point I am making here is General Semantics not only requires an intellectual commitment but, as George Kelly says, an involvement of the whole self in relation to the world around us.

Through the years I had attempted to, in a very haphazard fashion, utilize the first generation tools and techniques in General Semantics — dealing mostly with the what index, the where index, the who index, the how much index, etc., the hyphen and dating. Hayakawa's "Language in Thought and Action" laid the groundwork for those tools. This was before I read "Science and Sanity" by Korzybski. After reading "Science and Sanity" and "People in Quandaries" by Wendell Johnson, I was able to add to my "arsenal" of tools — in toolbox fashion: multi-ordinality, self-reflexiveness, non-allness, non-identity, the structural differential, non-elementalian and the General Semantics Epistemological framework as conceived by Korzybski. He emphasized in his second "Introduction to Science and Sanity" that dealing with the operating principles, i.e., the etc., indexes, dating, hyphens and quotes we could better extensionalize our theoretical knowledge; we could close the gap, somewhat, between the metaphysical and the empirical; between the world of practice and the world of theory. While the extensional principles worked pretty well, I realized later, much later as a matter of fact, after being exposed to Dr. Bois' latest development, that those concepts were rather static, difficult to internalize, to the extent necessary for effectiveness. I was like a carpenter carrying around a bag of tools, without a plan, waiting for someone to ask me to build a house. Later, I became an architect, as well as the carpenter, by combining first generation tools and techniques with the second generation's tools and techniques — which go into the other dimension Korzybski mentioned, our culture.

I must say, here, that while the first generation tools and techniques are found to be somewhat static, they are still useful and are a part of the total formulation, but, we must use them with that in mind. The static discovery does not render Korzybski obsolete. It only makes you pay more attention to his admonition that much more research needs to be done, in many areas, and he even spelled out the areas; and, that General Semantics Epistemology is a self-correcting body of knowledge which speaks to change and revamping of the notions contained within the framework. He emphasized, further, that by holding as fundamental the process of abstracting, non-identity and non-allness — the self-correcting mechanism would be automatic; but, this too can be held as tentative, if we are truly "Agents of Change."

When I began to relate to the second generation tools and techniques, I experienced a semantic jump. A semantic jump is when we begin to view things differently and the whole order of thinking is changed; when we begin to experience differently and new dimensions are added to our lives. At this point I began to relate to General Semantics as a "semantic reactor," i.e., one which is not just a thinking machine, an intellectual machine, but, a "reactive and transactive organism" "thinking," if you will, with feelings, the body organs, transcending logic, and rote memory. By doing this we reach another dimension, this is an example of the structural more, when we add the factors I mentioned. They are combined to form not only additions to an arsenal of tools and techniques — but, a different order of living — a new structure to life, and a new dimension in experiencing. So, we are not talking about adding, but multiplying. Geometric and non-additive type relationships which have given rise to concepts like non-additivity, span of control and the structural more in the social sciences and specifically in public administration and management.

So, we have, at this point, not only the intellectual equipment, and thinking level involvement, but a dimension which involves man in the total process of living. If you will notice I speak of living and not existing, living speaks to creating and human potential. The former speaks to survival which gives the impression of a "plodding" from day to day, a life of not only quiet but violent desperation. I believe what I am saying here can represent in some manner the processes of designing and creating, transforming and emerging, transacting and evolving, and self renewing and process.

My Contemporary Process

At the same time I relate as best I can to the theory of self reflexiveness, I take into account first order abstractions and blend with an operational and transactional knowing at the second order level. (For a full explanation of this see Weinberg, "Levels of Knowing and Existence.") Bois states it this way — $self_1$, $self_2$, and $self_3$ are different levels and an understanding of the operation determines situational action, based on a broad frame of reference experienced or felt in first order and non-verbal terms. I utilize extensional devices (etc., dates, indexes) and safety devices (quotes and hyphens), I distinguish between symbol and signal reactions. I note the non-intellectual aspects of semantic transacting. I pursue the idea of a structural unconscious, become more familiar with the structural more, become more aware of semantic jumps, utilize semantic psychoanalysis, and I move into the second generation semantic spectrum which boasts of five stages. They are: sensing-uncritical stage of the primitive classifying — the stage of labeling, introduced by Greek philosophers; relating — the power balance stage, the overarching and postulating stage, and the stage of relativity; and, the unifying and participating stage — the stages where we begin to experience creative activity based on the proper utilization of the General Semantics Epistemological process — the Quantum stage — this is called the Epistemological profile. The total process leading to the experiencing of the Zen and existential process. It enables me to practice in a systematic manner the kinds of things that may be automatic in eastern cultures. The total process along with the Epistemological profile moves me to a new level of practicing the art of awareness. The Epistemological profile, especially, enables me to understand the usefulness and levels of the various concepts within the General Semantics process, e.g., the indexes, multi-ordinality — I recognize, for example, that the indexes and multi-ordinality do not function at the postulating stage — because at that stage I am no longer being mostly analytical. I am a semantic transactor. The profile enables me to classify breeds of men, groups and individuals roughly according to the latest findings in General Semantics Epistemology. The Epistemological profile along with first generation tools and techniques enable me to systematically address myself to the value system I hold dear; I have also, with the tools, sharpened my research ability. I begin to see more systematically the development of the stages of our culture. This makes me a more effective time binder; puts me in closer touch with myself and my identity; and enables me to move to the unifying and participating stages.

My Specific Focus

I thought that public administration would benefit from a construct which directed the discipline to the midst of social action in the broadest sense thus, the application of the construct systemic-institutionalist to the field of public administration derived, in part, from General Semantics Epistemology. At least the emergence was brought about by exposure to the area. How does one, then, continue to formulate useful concepts or constructs, useful direction and effective action and management of self and the process?

The Process of Abstracting

By holding as fundamental the process of abstracting, I continue my journey, I abstract vertically and horizontally. It is a process by which I understand the world. It is a process by which I become aware of my surroundings. I utilize the construct of non-identity and non-allness. I tie them in with abstracting. This simply means that I am aware that I can only know a part of a thing from my own perspective. Not only that, I realize that my abstractions determine my relationships. Abstracting is a part of the foundation for the General Semantics process and threads throughout. The general awareness of this process gives us, as far as I know now, an understanding of the functioning of the human organism. If this be true, then we are close to the true functioning of our nervous system and thus the processes of the world. Abstracting is both lateral and vertical. The recognition of what level of abstracting we are on at any given time is basic to understanding our vertical operation. The recognition of our level lets me know how close I am to (WIGO)* and the level of inference I am on. It, also, tells me whether or not I am dealing with first or second order feelings and how I handle each. The crucial part is the diagnosis. Diagnosis, then is one of the most fundamental elements. The better the diagnosis, the more effective I become in managing myself and the situation. First of all, I admit that I do infer (abstract at all times) and conclude that the awareness of the process can improve the quality of my inferences, by virtue of first being aware of the process and by internalization of the process. This requires practice. I remember the map never does adequately represent the territory. (See Kenneth S. Keyes, Jr., "How to Develop Your Thinking Ability," for the best explanation of map vs. territory.)

I could devote many pages to this vertical process, but I think what I have said so far gives us an inkling. I do not have sufficient time or space to develop this portion of the General Semantics Epistemology fully. I will have to leave you on your own after a few brief examples.

* What Is Going On.

Abstracting: My Conceptual Re-Interpretation

My Notion of Vehicles

Let me take first the conceptual creative scheme conceived by Mary Parker Follett and put it to the test. How can I best operationalize the construct "law of the situation" by using the vertical abstracting process. First of all, my commitment should not be to the construct, concept, precept and pragmatic theories but to the highest abstract philosophical commitment which I choose to provide me with direction within the situation. The constructs, etc., are only vehicles for enabling me to realize the philosophical involvement. This is necessary for many reasons. The main one is that I must at all times be aware of where I am in the abstracting process. In other words, I do this to prevent myself from confusing means and ends and one level of abstracting with another. Automatically emerging out of this process is the equipment for automatic self correction of the vehicles, and the philosophical value frame of reference. This is a circular functioning mechanism not linear. As an example, let me start with a process that covers, fairly well, what I am talking about. The Center for Social Action, School of Public Administration, the field of public administration — The University of Southern California, Los Angeles City, Los Angeles County, State of California, the Nation, are vehicles enabling us to work within a larger frame of reference. Several things occur when I realize this: 1) I do not confuse lower means or goals with higher means or goals; 2) I do not become marooned at a lower level; 3) I view the problems differently; 4) I attack my problems differently; 5) I increase my options relative to what level can be used to obtain results; 6) I improve my chances for having a greater impact on the total situation.

Most of the above dictate what law prevails in each situation. Let me try to express this another way in talking style.

My Notion of Hoisting

The concept of vehicles, also, relates to the lateral or horizontal abstracting process. If I look upon our various operations as vehicles enabling us to accomplish a larger purpose — my options increase. The express purpose of what I am supposed to do at one level is broadened by what I have committed myself to at the highest level of the abstracting process. The by-products become as important as the aimed product. The concept of vehicles then is an example of the process of abstracting enabling me to develop new constructs for myself. I use one level to reach another level. The lower levels never become the ends in themselves. This brings me to the construct of hoisting. I hoist myself as I abstract. The construct of multiordinality is the mechanism for hoisting; it gives rise to the concept of hoisting. I rise to one level in order to look at another level.

Vehicles and Hoisting: Power

The constructs of vehicles and hoisting enable me not only to function at certain levels, but to become more effective in toto. Take the concept of power, for example. When the constructs of vehicles and hoisting are used I expand my power base. What I once viewed as low level, becomes more important when I use that lower level to reach another level. I do many more things with it than I normally would; thus, increasing my power in a position I thought contained no power. Anytime my options are increased and by-products are given as much consideration as the defined product, and tied in with the highest level of abstraction, which represents my overall philosophical commitment, I am utilizing the concept of multiordinality and at the same time increasing my power base and improving my significance as a functionary. I have more power than I realized when I begin to utilize the process of abstracting properly, along with efficient use of multiordinality — especially since it leads to constructs of vehicles and hoisting. By using this process, I operationalize the "law of the situation."

My Notion of Multi-ordinality

Multi-ordinality helps me to determine where I should function at a given time without "copping" out. Take the "black movement," for example, it is necessary at times to be very black, at another time it may be necessary to deal with the problem via the war in Vietnam, or all poor people, or all of humankind. The proper level of functioning is determined by my analysis of the situation, out of this emerges my level of attack. I am still working from my basic philosophy and frame of reference in a systematic fashion. I begin to co-join theory and practice — empirical and the metaphysical. In other words, I remain functional in a world where "copping" out is easy. I cannot attack the problem at the same level at all times.

Multi-ordinality can also be utilized to offset conflict — listen to this example: The Associate Director of the School of Public Administration and I had a very heated discussion, bordering on a bit of conflict, concerning a matter. As I look at the discussion in retrospect, there was no need for the heat or the conflict. We were confusing our levels of abstracting. He was discussing the matter from the standpoint of operations; I wanted to discuss it from the level of "politics." Neither of us were wrong, they were separate issues on two different levels. A useless conflict situation was created. If we had taken pause to discuss it in terms of the multi-ordinal framework, radial energy could have been saved.

Many of our conflicts come about because we confuse the levels. Multi-ordinality is useful in helping us to recognize where we are.

I Order My General Semantics Epistemological World

I order my world in several different ways. They all, however, relate to my overarching commitment and philosophical frame of reference.

One basic way I organize my world is by relating to the metaphysical and empirical worlds. I relate to them in my own fashion; I develop an understanding *My Metaphysical and Empirical Worlds.*

I consider, for example, the empirical world the objective abstracting world and put the metaphysical in the classifying abstracting world. I insist that when I talk I am referring to two different worlds. I see the metaphysical as the "make believe world," the "theoretical" and the dream world — the ought and what might be world. In that world I create categories, not as I see them but as I think they are. I try to move beyond the empirical to the silent level or better still the submicroscopic level — the level where things are not seen but exist. I see the two worlds as not separate; they are similar up to a point, and at this point the empirical is transformed into the metaphysical. All along, however, the metaphysical has been operating in transaction. This is where I reside as a social scientist.

My major concern is to make the transition from one world to the other orderly and recognize when they are not separate. In the latter case I am talking about them side by side — especially when I am relating to more abstract, empirical relationships. The classic case is the American Constitution, which talks about what ought to be empirically. My problem is always to separate the metaphysical symbolism from the empirically abstract relationships that actually do exist and might be. In cases of this type it is difficult for me to separate the empirical from the metaphysical; consequently, my objective and classifying abstracting will not provide the clues for identifying the neat little worlds I have set up to give me direction. But, the categories are convenient for analysis. Said another way, I may be talking about a metaphysical world which is dealing with "abstract (not concrete) empiricism" and which utilizes classifying abstracting instead of objective abstracting, as is usually the case, when we relate to the empirical world.

I roughly evaluate my worlds with the Epistemological profile. I see objective abstracting, in the empirical world. I see concrete empirical things, as having a cut-off point at the postulating stage of the Epistemological profile and moving metaphysically into classifying abstracting in order to provide a jump to the postulating and unifying stages (conceptual activity). I see classifying abstracting as beginning at any stage and moving automatically into the unifying stage — stage five, the stage of experiences and revelations. In this case, classifying abstracting — the empirical abstract-non-concrete world, the semantic jump does not take place. I am abstracting with precision and without interruption from the sensing stage to the unifying stage and participating level of that stage. I see abstracting playing the role of moving up and down the abstracting ladder; and up and down the Epistemological profile until the unifying stage assumes control. This is where my semantic jumps take place.

In short, what I do for the most part is classify, classifying metaphysical "abstracting" as a different order of things. I move it under the heading of the Epistemological profile. In the case of objective empirical abstracting, I think about multi-ordinality and the process of abstracting about things of the same order, having an empirical relationship that only becomes metaphysical when the empiricism begins to phase into the non-verbal.

This orders my world and allows me to relate personally to the General Semantics Epistemological process.

The Autobiography of a Construct: a Stage Five Experience

An Experience

The processes I have described thus far are "part and parcel" of my New York experience.

What I Knew

I lived for many years knowing intellectually that things were related. That if you touched one part of something it affected and had an impact on the whole. I knew intellectually, also, that knowing on that level is one thing; but, knowing that you knew was the act of being aware of your awareness.

I knew intellectually that our "system," at least that part of it which dehumanizes the "spirit" and the divine potential of man, was wrong and needed revamping and the instituting of revolutionary changes, not just reform. Revolutionary changes I am talking about here, have as much to do with cultural thinking and behavioral changes, as physical changes, which operate within the old premises, values and framework.

What Happened

As I was walking down 14th Street that day, my whole life loomed up before me and I saw myself emerging through a burst cloud. It was a bright sunny day in New York, but the brightness I saw was a brightness I had never seen in ordinary light. It was a "spiritual" light. My intellectual thoughts at that moment became a part of my being. I knew at that moment what my dedication was. I knew what I would die for. I felt, deep down, on the level where we all live, that the system had to go or man was doomed. Not just black man, red man, yellow man, but white men and all humans. I felt for the first time the dangers of non-creative living and just living to exist and survive.

I saw and felt vividly the expression "system" — which eventually gave rise to the construct of "systemic institutionalist." I saw an overarching philosophical framework take shape which put everything into some kind of order and place, including death and friends. They all fell within a broader philosophical framework which transcended my every day life. I saw the black movement as part of a greater movement. Thus, an impelling force to move beyond race to human kind in order to find solutions to problems. It represented not a love for one race but human kind. That day I became a human being in addition to a black man. I knew my blackness had its place and would continue to be emphasized in terms of identity; but, within a broader framework of revolutionary human kindness at one level and a transactional reality at another level. I knew I would not only die for the plight of black people but any man be he white, black or otherwise, seeking to become a new breed of man and holding a certain set of values. I knew that this type of person had a lease on my life. At this level my commitment knows no color. I committed myself to the concept of Breeds of men.

I suppose we could do as George Kelly did and call this the autobiography of a theory. I have shared this personal experience with you in order to illustrate what in my mind, internalizing the General Semantics Epistemological process means. I have tried to say that relating to the process requires not only "intellectual equipment" — I mean that in the sense of not being feeble minded — but, a commitment and involvement. A *living* and *practicing* of the philosophical premises as well as the methodology. It is an every day affair, discouraging at times, but rewarding in terms of outcome.

Conclusion

By utilizing this methodology, I believe I can move into the process world, discard obsolete models, discard the static noun and begin to behave as a "transaction in process." Moreover, move conceptual activity to the "nitty gritty."

Without an overarching system, allied with proper methodology, it becomes next to impossible to comprehend the total pattern and the group activity of a huge mass of semi-autonomous elements as we have in the field of public administration.

Our task is to illuminate the goals, if we are to give directions and address ourselves to the recommendations emerging out of Crestline. We must give shape and scope for self direction and creativity. If our goals are too narrowly or too vaguely defined or too forbiddingly presented, we will mold our people into mere cogs in a mass production machine.

If we are to address ourselves to the Harris Paper, regarding the Ken Smith Proposal, we must take a semantic jump and define our activity in abstractions high enough to meaningfully embrace the various levels of our activity. "Systemic-institutionalist" is merely the first step along that long road. Our responsibility is more and our capacities and potential are greater. We are in a transacting process which defies description at this time. With faith in the fact that man can make himself, we can sharpen our definition of where we ought to be — and develop a construct of where we might be.

No one said it was easy. It is a process in transaction, requiring the mastering and practicing of the latest in the General Semantics Epistemology, and the developing of a set of philosophical values projecting public administration into universal movement and transaction.

Finally, unless our focus is large and comprehensive, our contributions will be insignificant. For our problems are world problems; our concerns are universal concerns. Unless we can relate our "cubby hole" to a larger context, frustration, dissatisfaction, lack of hope and discouragement become themes by which we live.

We can begin by being transactive instead of reactive — as Ramos puts it, pro-active. This will be the beginning of moving us into the third generations. This, hopefully, will enable us to initiate constructs that give us a radical new "feel." Constructs that will provide new directions both in Public Administration and General Semantics Epistemology. The introduction to the third generation is being provided by Dr. J. Samuel Bois in his new book — which will either be titled "Organic Philosophy" or "New Directions." These new directions will include symbols and a language which will enable many of us to become less secular; to build an equation that is more fluid and relate to symbols that raise us to new levels of involvement. The notions of "Transactions in Process" and the "Central Assembly" are basic to these New Directions.

CHAPTER VI

THE SEMANTIC REACTOR-THEORY - PRACTICE, GROWTH - CHANGE

Occasional Paper Number One

Introduction

The purposes of this paper are: (1) to discuss one of the key methodologies, tools, or techniques (classified herein as a concept) within the General Semantics Epistemological Process; (2) to attempt to show how deep involvement with this methodology enables us to synthesize theoretical and practical concerns; and, how that synthesis produces a self-correcting mechanism, promotes the invention of workable constructs, new tools for self-management and direction. So. I begin.

The Semantic Reactor: Theory-Practice

If a person is truly a semantic reactor then the why question and causation will become secondary considerations or negative consequences will occur. The fear of reductionism "boils" down, for the most part, to focusing consciously or unconsciously on the question of why and what caused it. You see, at this point we are speaking of one cause and it reduces our chances of feeling and being aware of the total situation. In situations regarding immediate decisions the construct of semantic reactor is a most important one; and, in situations regarding the joining of practice and theory the construct, semantic reactor, is significant. In these situations we almost never try to find one cause or find out why, but accept the fact that something is happening to us and our whole being is involved. Many times, for example, we say the weather is bad; therefore, we feel bad — one cause — or if we had had a different room things would have gone differently — one cause. Perhaps, in both cases we may be correct, but, it is only one element. When we indulge in this, we are in the midst of reductionism and this kind of reductionism is totally unfit for humankind. We can only rise to a new level of understanding of the total situation if we regard ourselves as a semantic reactor. At that point we realize we are in the middle of the situation and allow all of our being to interpret and feel. Thus, two things occur: (1) we have a better chance of making a decision we never dreamed of; and (2) we begin to build a theoretical frame of reference at a significant, high, level which allows us to transfer our reductions to similar situations.

One of the serious consequences of not being a semantic reactor, not understanding in verbal and non-verbal terms, is we classify what's taking place in terms of low level terminology; for example, I am paranoid today, I am depressed — this kind of interpretation of our behavior maroons us at the classifying stage (stage of labeling — a thing is what we say it is) of the epistemological profile. We judge ourselves harshly and we are unable to build that meaning about our lives which makes us significant and which would enable us to do away with low level psychological notions. The opposite occurs when we become a semantic reactor: (1) our decision-making ability is improved; (2) we become self-actualizing; (3) we do away with notions that constrain us; (4) the low level notions begin to fade into the background, and (5) we become a transcending person, building sufficient abstract concepts that enable us to operate as theoretic practitioners with surprising ease.

We in the social sciences, especially Public Administration, have a tendency to shy away from abstract theory. We say we classify ourselves as practitioners or empirical theorists — not realizing on a feel level that we are operating on the basis of some kind of abstract personal construct at all times which we cannot separate from hard empiricism. Our failing is that we are not aware of that construct and we certainly do not know at what level it is. By becoming a semantic reactor (a person who synthesizes within an overarching framework) we raise the level of our theory-making ability, we see and embrace more and our chances of being accurate as well as adequate are improved. We then, in a systematic fashion, become aware of our theory-making ability and we no longer falsely separate the two. Theory and practice become a part of our doing. We become artistic, as most scientists are, and creative. The joining of theory and practice makes artists out of us. We are no longer just the carpenter but the architect also. We make our professions and doings artistic. We bring a certain flair to the most mechanistic of endeavors.

Humankind's ability to manage (you see I say humans, this way I include women who should not be left out — the moment we say man unconsciously we do not include women, but this is another story and has to be dealt with in another paper) depends upon our concept of humans. Our concept must be total; and, placing ourselves within the realm of the semantic reactor gives us a broader and deeper understanding. It, at once, becomes a concept within the General Semantics epistemologic framework and process, which not only holds the key to what man may be, but a method by which he attains on a daily, and long range basis, that philosophical frame of reference that speaks to significance and the meaning of life. The critical point here is that the various concepts within the General Semantics epistemological process join theory and practice. They are, at once, the philosophy and the methodology. Our major task, and it is an important one, is to internalize the concept to the degree that it becomes a personal construct. From that flows the how and the vehicles for actions. We cannot speak of transcending, understanding phenomena and joining of theory and practice, until we have concepts that are rich and fertile enough; to enable us to reach that philosophical state where we think humans ought and might be.

Being in the field of Public Administration I would naturally think of practical-everyday tools — how one bridges the gap and moves into the action stage. If we start with the assumption that there is no gap — then there is nothing to bridge. How then do we look at the world, then what do we do? I take the position that we abstract and a consciousness of that process is important. It is a vertical process. A major difference between the theoretician and practitioner is that one stops and thinks about the process and the other does not to the same extent. The practitioner cannot take the time to reflect and build a conscious overarching systematic approach. His level of abstraction, therefore, may be low, many times, because the situation does not call for high abstract theory but middle range one situational theory. But, with the proper synthetic approach and a process like overarching theoretical framework, the practitioner synthesizes and is able to develop within his frame of reference, constructs, that cover situations rather than a situation on an ongoing and automatic basis. A firm separation of values and empiricism puts us "smack" in the camp of the logical-positivist and our chances of internalizing a theoretical framework are lessened. At the same time our chances of building a self-corrective system which synthesizes our synthetic worlds and enables theory and practice to act upon one another, are improved.

The process I am referring to here requires practice. We internalize and practice the various methodologies within the General Semantics process. One such methodology is the semantic reactor. In order to internalize — process wise — the semantic reactor, it is necessary to move from "intellectual" concept to "transactive" construct.

The Semantic Reactor: From Concept to Construct

When one goes through a period of creative confusion — it is a prelude to a discovery, if the person recognizes the "state" as a creative experience and sees himself as a semantic reactor, his understanding is expanded and the words, why — and cause — become secondary elements to the total experience. Example, after completing my fifth position paper, I had a dream, I visualized the concept of growth and change — after the visualization the concept of growth became a construct. It became a construct because, I began to "feel" the concept of growth — and until we begin to feel a concept it remains a concept — when we feel it, it becomes a personal construct and we are ready to manage ourselves and situations with it.

Simultaneously, I went through a phase which I described to myself as a lull, this lasted for about five days. I felt confused and "unsure" less "confident" and muddled about what I thought I knew, things did not hang together well, and I was using old terminology to explain a creative confused state or "pre-creative" excitement. As long as I was describing it as depressive or some other low level psychological state, it kept me marooned at the lowest abstract level. The moment I began to view it as a semantic reactor and related it to creativity I began to emerge. As I entered into the sixth day I realized I was searching for new meaning and new significance. When this became clear I started writing this — my first occasional paper. I have shared this experience for one main reason: we suffer from what Logotherapy describes as an existential vacuum. Logotherapy views man as a responsible creature who must actualize the potential meaning of life. It stresses that the true meaning of life is to be found in the world rather than within man or his psyche; and, that human existence is essentially self transcending rather than self-actualizing. Man's concern, even his despair over the worthwhileness of life, is a spiritual distress and not a mental disease. It may require the piloting of a person through a growth and development stage rather than burying or marooning a person at a sensing stage of the (stage of the primitive) epistemological profile where he becomes an analytical agent of whys and causes for "Normal Neurotic" tendencies. (More on this can be obtained from Viktor E. Frankl's "Man's Search for Meaning: An Introduction to Logotherapy," especially under the section labeled basic concepts of logotherapy, p. 151).

To seek this meaning to life is, in my judgment, a revolutionary concept in psychotherapy and raises it to the highest abstract level and supplies man with an overarching theory to live by. It remains, as so many high level abstractions, without major significance — unless we do two things: (1) systematically practice theoretical integration and construct genuine functional interconnections between theories and/or constructs; (2) develop methodology that can be internalized and be reasonably in conformance with the highest ideals we specify for humankind. This way growth will occur and the dynamics of change are no longer considered "foreign" agents. I specify and pinpoint in this paper one such construct, the *semantic reactor*. In addition to tying in with the ideals, the goals, and the meaning the purpose and being the meaning, the semantic reactor is also a methodology. It is a construct of sufficiently high level to embrace this ideal and is sufficiently flexible to operate at the operational level in terms of enabling us to practice transcendence and awareness. We continue to seek a meaning in our life — and we go through these creative stages and confused states, to do it. The way we define them will determine how we handle them or what happens as we move through this muddled state. If we define it in low level psychological terms our results will be low level and may make us ready for the "nut house." If we raise the level of our thinking to the fourth level (postulating level — tentativeness and relativity) of the Epistemological Profile, our chances of realizing the unifying stage and having a creative experience are improved.

The semantic reactor construct enables us to combine theory and practice. It embraces more and enables us to "practice what we preach." It improves our decision making ability, we subscribe to transcendence — and things way beyond self-actualization.

The Semantic Reactor: The Maturing of a Construct

I had been familiar with the concept of growth but never really associated it with the label change — the moment it became a construct — after my visualization — I started using it in relation to change. As I moved within the unifying stage to the participating level of that stage — I started consciously analyzing the process of change which I was now relating to through a construct. I no longer considered the concept of change the most favored way of relating to a dynamic process we are seeking to understand. I have come to the basic conclusion that change did not necessarily mean growth although used in that sense primarily. This may be one reason for the question, change for and to what? It is a legitimate question when we realize that change could mean moving from one side of a room to another side of a room to change from deduction-induction to induction-deduction. Both are logical combinations within the Aristotelian system. This represents a change, but without a difference which makes a difference, there is no real movement. The kind of change we are speaking about must involve differences and represent a major emphasis on being non-static. The concept and now the construct of growth specifies the kind of change we wish to see. This way we are able to feel growth and visualize it on the abstracting ladder. Growth, then, enables us to specify and move the concept of change into vertical activity. Change then becomes an upward process and it gives us sufficient focus and direction.

As a semantic reactor, combining all of the "ologies" and energies of the universe, we join theory and practice without consciously thinking of it.

Again: our major concern is whether or not we are growing within an overarching framework which recognizes man as a time binder and semantic reactor. And, whether or not we build an epistemological process which gives sufficient meaning to our lives. Moreover, that this meaning is overarching and will enable the how to flow from the what, in terms of immediate and long range decisions; and, will enable us to embrace theoretical concerns in a systematic fashion. In addition, enable us to hang our notions and concepts and other notions together in a fashion that formulates meaningful relationships of the findings sequestered within our own and other disciplines. Thus, a semantic reactor has, according to Bois, at least seven aspects or dimensions, they are: thinking, feeling, self-moving, electro, chemical, environmental, past and future. If I add the "ologies" (psychology, sociology, biology and anthropology) in a non-stratigraphic fashion the description is more complete. It is not necessary that we remember the ingredients of the semantic reactor — except for conversation and research purposes. It is more important that we become open enough to transform this concept into a construct; meaning that we internalize the concept by moving to the non-verbal level at which point it becomes a personal construct. Again, we join empiricism and metaphysics, fact and value, theory and practice. The synthesizing of these, moves us away from logical positivism into the arena of creativity, change and action.

The Semantic Reactor: A Summary Note

The construct, Semantic Reactor, enables us to replace the stratigraphic conception of the relations between the various aspects of human existence with a synthetic one; that is, biology, sociology, psychology, and anthropology are treated as variables within a unitary system. This way we are able to integrate different types of concepts and theories in such a way that we are a party to the emergence of new constructs. The emergence or transformation of concepts into constructs lends legitimately to the idea that it is not a matter of coining new terminology; but, it speaks to whether or not we can take old concepts that reveal the enduring natural processes and transform them into personal constructs. We, naturally, under these circumstances, combine theory and practice automatically within us as a semantic reactor. The transformation, itself, which gives rise to the personal construct moves from the semantic reactor position to the semantic transactor position — the process is *movement*. By using the semantic reactor we cease to feel mediocre, accidental and mortal — we get a sudden insight into meaning. Man as a semantic reactor provides hope for man — it is an optimistic philosophy as well as an optimistic methodology. The General Semantics Epistemology founded on such concepts frees itself of running into a cul de sac as existentialism has, or Zen Buddhism might and as phenomenology is proving to do — if the static concepts are not revised and methodologies are not developed.

Our capacity to synthesize theory and practice is determined, to some extent, by our ability to develop conceptual schemes of sufficient range, depth, magnitude and multi-dimensionality that relate parts in a coherent fashion. A direct result is the automatic improvement of our decision-making. I am talking about the appropriate decision emerging out of the situation. This becomes a self-reflexive and non-thinking process. A reactive and transactive process. It does not require the consciously calling for of ideas; it requires continuous building of the process within the theoretical frame in a self-corrective manner.

Our semantic reactor operating within the total General Semantics Epistemological process reminds us that we should take a closer look at phenomena, concepts, theories, definitions, and ways of functioning; we are able to do this because the nature of the process requires that we continue to look at new ideas in a process-like fashion. The process implicitly requires us to continue searching simply because it is a process orientation. For example, the notion of regression (there are others but I'll just take this one in order to clarify the point) is outmoded. We know now that people do not "regress" as such, it is the kind of growth that may be taking place as they may have moved to another level, but not in keeping with the kind of changes that speak to man as an effective time binder. The values may be based on old notions and old ways of looking at new phenomena and changes. Consequently, at a certain point they seem out of step. The notion of "regression" does not accurately or adequately explain what is taking place. And, our interpretations and diagnoses dictate the solutions or attitudes we apply to dealing with everything from a lowly employee by a public administrator, to the kind of treatment prescribed in the field of psychotherapy. In other words our map should represent the territory. The crucial question is how do we begin to question and know these things on an automatic basis. One answer is becoming familiar and aware of the General Semantics Epistemological process and internalizing the various methodologies. One such methodology, tool or technique I have discussed in this paper is humankind as a semantic reactor, this may provide a beginning.

Other constructs will be developed and written about as I introduce the various methodologies within the General Semantics Epistemological process. The semantic reactor is just one within the total framework. It was first introduced by Korzybski in 1933 and expanded upon by Bois in 1966.

CHAPTER VII

MULTI-ORDINALITY IN ACTION

Occasional Paper Number Two

Multi-Ordinality as a Process

One of the major weaknesses may be our inability to recognize changes when they have occurred. Being members of the present cultural setting; and being a product of yesterday's cultural milieu we are automatically, each one to a different degree and in some cases a different manner — maybe representing a difference in kind — a product of the past-present-future, therefore, our models, concepts and personal constructs are structured accordingly. We attempt to apply these models, concepts and personal constructs to the present situations as un-updated, revised and unchanged. Usually they are not "good" analytical agents of what is taking place. What is the answer then? One answer is to adopt a method that will update us and revise our concepts, models, and personal constructs automatically. This note, then, brings me to another concept, model, analytical tool, or methodology, within the General Semantics Epistemological framework. That methodology is multi-ordinality. As you may recall; in my first occasional paper I talked about the Semantic reactor as a methodology within the General Semantics Epistemological process. Multi-ordinality is another such methodology. It does not cover the same territory as the semantic reactor does. The semantic reactor concept is more embracing and can be considered the nerve center for most or all of the tools, techniques, and methodologies within the Epistemological process; even the Epistemological profile and the third generation transaction attitudes.

Multi-ordinality is confined mainly to levels of abstracting — in other words, it is a methodology for aiding us in understanding the vertical process of abstracting, once we have come to a decision about a concept or construct. In this case — for example, the construct of growth, as discussed in my first occasional paper — the multi-ordinality methodology or concept enables us to experientially and experimentally examine the construct of growth, relative to validity and relevancy to the concept of change.

If we apply the concept of multi-ordinality to the construct of growth, in analytical terms, we find that on the very lowest level growth means, in the biological sense, the very beginning of an idea as in conception. Once the idea of growth is implanted as in conception, we go through a process of nurturing — then we move to a second level — the level of being born; in the case of the idea, it is the level of discovery; we have a vague feeling that we are on the right track — although nothing concrete can be said except that we are "open." In the third phase we begin to see and imagine the body developing and the submicroscopic mental-physical processes taking place. In the case of the construct of growth, we experience new meanings regarding change — we begin to experience change in a vertical sense; growth becomes an instrument by which we measure the extent to which we have moved from, say the example of, the administrator or teacher having the last word in a discussion to a more group-like process, and so on. We could continue in this fashion until we reach a higher level of inference, about the growth of a particular construct or a particular program; or the lack of growth of a particular program or idea. Is there any value in this type of approach, in view of the fact that we would like to make geometric, quantum and revolutionary changes in order to provide the necessary direction for ourselves and society? Well, several things come to mind: (1) the concept supplies us with a theoretical frame of reference for automatically analyzing situations — it is structural in nature and can give us insight into what we are doing; (2) it can help us in determining at what level we are operating — on the abstracting ladder — at a given time, whether we are relating to the construct of growth or the concept of conflict, change, love or power, etc. In other words, multi-ordinality aids us in locating ourselves in relation to the target; and, in addition to that, pinpoints the "bull's-eye"; (3) it makes us more effective time-binders. It gives us a clue, in an overall sense, as to how much and how little has been done, what level it has been done on and what needs to be done. It tends to make our "map of the territory" adequate as well as accurate; (4) it keeps us from making a "fool" out of ourselves and enables us to build a more complete case; and, (5) it is, most of all a prelude to action — not the action itself.

After the analytical process has taken place — again I am not talking about this in a logical sense or mechanical sense; but, in terms of internalization which enables us to diagnose situations automatically — either on the "spot" or in "reflection." In either case it becomes a worthwhile methodology. We decide upon our mode of action, it may be revolutionary, reforming, or, a decision that the process going as it is, is satisfactory. Whatever tactic we decide upon doesn't emerge out of ignorance of the situation. It is a process which, in many cases may give us immediate insight. Without a sound theoretical frame of reference or process we cannot begin to synthesize and eliminate the false dichotomy of theory and practice. It becomes — as you can see, as it blends — a "creative" process for decision-making.

I was speaking at Benedict College in Columbia, South Carolina, in March of 1970, at their 1970 Black Economic Development Conference — I tried as best I could to convey the value of internalizing this process. In the question and answer period it became a rather trying experience. As I tried to relate to them what I thought the value of this was — I constantly got the feedback that I must have some "mystical power," they agreed with the concept; but, we had difficulty developing how the process could be applied to a particular situation. This is a normal difficulty, especially when one tries to move from the pure "intellectual" nuts and bolts to a creative process which relates to listening to our inner world and then trying to convey what has taken place or the "voices" we have heard. This is referred to as "mystical." There is not much mysticism about it. It is merely moving the decision-making process from the mechanical analytical world (concept) to the non-verbal synthetic world (personal construct). But, to convey this without indulging in a process makes one at times feel "silly."

One panelist at Benedict — it was somewhat amusing, and delightful but frustrating — constantly referred to the mysticism and ended his talk by saying that he could only think of one way for bringing about change, that was through "confrontation." Precisely, his lack of a theoretical frame or process and the lack of understanding of the concept multi-ordinality marooned him at this level. He neither had a tool nor methodology for providing horizontal or vertical analysis which would provide options of attack regarding very complex problems. Implicit in his remark was, I am rendering myself ineffective when confrontation is not appropriate; also, my ability to automatically develop new constructs to meet new changes and growth, is limited.

The concept of multi-ordinality enables us to move into action at different levels with different tactics if warranted — achieving over-all results. And, we do not provide ourselves with an excuse for "copping" out; nor do we design a failure situation (to borrow a phrase from Professor John Gerletti) for ourselves. Instead we move to a different level with a different tactic which comes automatically to mind by utilizing the concept of multi-ordinality. Consequently, we do not fail, we have accomplished objectives which are by-products. In other words, our attainment may be more "symbolic" than "tangible." The point is we know — hence we do not impose erroneous value judgments on what has taken place.

One must have a meaning in his life, he must feel significant, he must have a sense of success — in order not to become immobilized and discouraged in a world requiring an on-going commitment to a process — multi-ordinality internalized is one way of moving in this direction. It is a matter of moving from learning to knowing, which is a difference that makes a difference.

CHAPTER VIII

EXTENSIONALIZATION BRIDGES THE GAP BETWEEN THEORY AND PRACTICE

Occasional Paper Number Three

Extensionalization as a Process

Extensionalization is the link between theory and practice of General Semantics epistemology — Korzybski said, "the difference between people in the mental hospitals and those out, is that one extensionalizes and one does not" (the former intensionalizes).

The best way, perhaps, to express extensionalization is through the general synthetic set-up of theory versus practice or observation versus inference.

A friend of mine was visiting his mother and was about to leave to see a movie when his mother began to complain that she was lonely. He decided, after some thought, to cancel his movie engagement and instead asked his date to sit along with him while he kept his mother company. The mother announced fifteen minutes later that she was going out. He was taken aback because he had assumed that this was what she wanted; he did not extensionalize his theory, he took action without posing a proper question.

In another instance this same person was going to take his grandmother to the airport to have a plane ticket re-written. I informed the person that the drive to the airport would be unnecessary and the same thing could be accomplished by contacting a travel agency in the neighborhood by phone. I was informed that the grandmother would not consider doing it in that manner. Later that day I received a phone call saying that the situation had been explained to the grandmother and she had agreed to do it re: the travel agency. He had inferred that the grandmother was committed to going to the airport. The person extensionalized by eventually checking out their theory or inference. It saved several hours and enabled both of them to accomplish other things that seemed to have been running in conflict with the airport trip.

We reach many conclusions or develop theories based on inferences; we can only be more certain that our theories are correct if we extensionalize. Inferences are theories; theories must be checked out.

This provides the empirical aspect of the General Semantics epistemological process. We become aware of extensionalizing — at the same time we realize that we cannot check out all theories immediately and in the same manner. The best we can do is realize that the value of inferences can only be determined after adequate extensionalization. As long as we are aware that extensionalization has not taken place we can determine the risk involved in our theoretical undertaking. We are constantly developing this kind of process. The crucial point is to be aware that we are involved in this type of process.

Whether using first, second, or third generation tools, techniques, or methodologies, extensionalization becomes one of the fundamental concepts and major backdrops for all of the methodologies.

When, for example, we are using multi-ordinality, the epistemological profile, the laws of non-identity and non-allness, semantic-reactor abstracting, etc., our conclusions, theories, and inferences must be checked out; and, because of the systematic relationship and the embracing implications of each methodology, the selection of one of any of the methodologies will automatically stimulate the working of the other appropriate methodology at the proper time. For example, the construct of growth I have spoken about, in other papers, whether it is examined through multi-ordinality or the epistemological profile; we constantly utilize the concept of extensionalization to check out the conclusions reached relative to the construct of growth as being the key to the concept of change. When examined in terms of the epistemological profile we develop the theory that when growth reaches the unifying stage of the profile we begin to relate more to creativity and we operationalize this creativity at the participating level of the unifying stage. The participating level becomes our extensional device. The circular functioning of the General Semantics epistemology process, when used as a theoretical methodology, set in motion the automatic corrective mechanism enabling us to revise, restructure, revamp and replace our original notions. That automatic self correcting mechanism threading throughout the process is extensionalization.

Keys to understanding the role of extensionalization are as follows: First, we do not extensionalize in an awareness manner (and I say awareness because we are always extensionalizing; it is an automatic functioning of our semantic reacting and transacting process. But, we, for the most part, do not extensionalize in a scientifically artistic and systematic fashion, i.e., with heightened awareness) for we are afraid to check out inferences and theories from which we might receive feedback which will do violence to the values and notions we hold dear. The morning I became aware that my two and a half year old daughter was not very friendly to me I wondered whether I was correct or was just feeling "overly sensitive." After deliberating for a moment I decided to test it out. I said, "Come on and kiss Daddy." She replied, "Oh no," and ran away and ignored me the rest of the morning. My wife said, "I see you like punishment." I was hurt but I felt as if I had displayed a modicum of "courage" by forcing the issue. This is a relatively harmless example. The point I am trying to make is: there are psychological problems connected with extensionalizing. Once we are aware of this, and begin to deal with this factor, our ability to extensionalize is improved and becomes more scientifically artistic. The "open" and "aware" person is a better extensionalizer.

Second, we must be aware that in order to extensionalize properly, we must understand the limitations and under what circumstances extensionalization is possible. Extensionalization, at the moment, can be characterized in the following manner: 1) Unverifiable theories, i.e., Is God dead? Is there a heaven? What came first, the chicken or the egg? These are unanswerable and unverifiable questions that do not lend themselves to extensionalization. So, semantically we do not bother with such questions unless we just want to play games and have fun. We are very much in the world of intensionalization and pure "metaphysic." 2) Verifiable theories — e.g., How many bricks are in that pile? How many houses are on that street? How many students are in this class? 3) Unverified verifiable theories — this has to do with time. It is probably our most complex area and the one which receives much of our attention. It is unquantifiable. Let me take a personal example to illustrate this. After writing my first position paper, I was asked to speak to a group of graduate students regarding General Semantics and Phenomenology. I had a hunch that this was not the best thing to do. I thought it best to first lay some groundwork by writing additional papers, in order to explain my position, have the students and others read them and then have a discussion. I thought another approach would not only do violence to the field of General Semantics, but it would also leave most of us frustrated if we did not first communicate some basic concepts that could not possibly be explained and examined orally. Without this process I foresaw a debate and defense of positions. Instead I wanted to create an atmosphere that would produce a discussion and a creative learning process. I thought this former procedure would. After the fifth position paper, a group of doctoral students arranged a series of seminars. I was slated to speak at one. The students had read the papers and were prepared for an exchange of ideas and a process where we would all be learners. This is exactly what took place. As a result General Semantics epistemology received a fair hearing and possibly gained some currency and relevance.

To capsule — I started with the theory that it was better to lay a foundation in writing in order to obtain the best results. I tested my theory by getting feedback on the individual papers and finally by the results of the seminar we were involved in. The final test of the correctness of my position was the seminar itself. This is one example of extensionalization which falls into the verifiable-unverified category, i.e., it took time to check out the theory based on the inference.

We make decisions every day on this basis — our decisions are theoretical inferences that, perhaps, cannot be verified at the moment. They are metaphysical — awaiting some type of empirical connection. Some other examples that fall into this category are — are they able to do the kind of job we expect? Will he make A's in college? Will she act this way in X situations? These remain theories, unextensionalized until verification takes place.

Another example is one verified recently. For a long time I was walking around with a tentative theory in my "unpure" metaphysical world based on a superficial analysis of the empirical world. I was of the opinion that the School of Public Administration at U.S.C. should set up a program to do the following: 1) inaugurate public administration programs at predominantly Black colleges, 2) set up institutes at Black institutions in the South to train political aspirants and those who were elected, on how to function in office, 3) set up a similar type of program for white public officials and aspiring candidates. (This led to the conclusion that we need, not just black leaders or white leaders but, leaders of a different breed, be they black or white.) In all instances, the major thrust would be to develop a new direction in social action; since we are badly in need of a new kind of leadership.

I spoke at Benedict College in South Carolina recently. They are striving to set up the kind of program mentioned above; but, they are in need of money and technical assistance. Since that time I have received information about other colleges in other areas. My extensionalization is somewhat complete — my theory or concept has now become a construct for action. This was an unverified verifiable theory which is now approaching being verified. My map now represents, to a greater extent, the territory.

Thirdly, there is another area which neither falls, wholly, within the intensional nor extensional processes. This may be classified as the area of unconscious intensional-extensional activity. It has to do primarily with conceptual activity that does not lend itself to logical analysis. It is high level abstract creativity, mostly on the non-verbal level. It may be referred to as "mysticism," "revelations," or "visions." The so-called pure scientist will call them "hunches," "intuitions," etc. This is where we are when our symbol-making activity is non-verbal and has no visible or even vague connections that we can count on, as being verifiable in terms of time and the future. The construct or theory comes to us by way of "feel." The crucial question is whether or not it is a sensing level experience (the first level of the epistemological profile) or a unifying experience (the fifth level of the epistemological profile). All we know is that it defies analysis in "normal" terms. Our major protective device is to hold the concept, theory or construct tentative until new epistemological findings are internalized which will give us additional insight into our non-verbal activity. This tentativeness represents the difference between the sensing stage and the unifying stage of the epistemological profile. This pinpoints the usefulness of the epistemological profile in providing a deeper understanding of the methodologies within the General Semantics Epistemological process: in this case extensionalization. It is a difference which makes a difference; and takes us a step beyond Korzybski's interpretation of extension and intension. However, by utilizing his "spiral theory" which ties in with man as time-binder, we begin to understand phenomena which, at the present time, have no scientific foundation.

This, inevitably, leads to the principle of probability, a principle to be acted upon from minute to minute, day in and day out. It is an awareness that we abstract not only verbally but non-verbally; and, that the non-verbal area has a check system of its own. It is the theory, held tentative of course, that we abstract beyond realms imaginable. It is the continual testing of one's beliefs, assumptions, and one's knowledge against non-verbal experiences.

Again, the one instrument which makes us dare to "dabble" with these non-verbal experiences and abstractions in a conscious sense and gives us courage to go where mortals fear to tread is the epistemological profile as designed by Dr. J. Samuel Bois. It is an attempt at defining and re-defining, in an automatic sense, these experiences; and, where we are in terms of abstracting. His profile is the continuation of modern epistemology which we must embrace if we are to understand. It enables us to continue to move from "pure learning" to "knowing." It is a 'difference which makes a difference.'

Fourthly, we must be aware of the way we pose questions if our extensionalization process is to work scientifically-artistic. The question is, "Will you put up with my erratic behavior during this period — can you take it?" The answer, "I don't know whether I can take it or not; I must know what you mean — can I take what?" In the first place the question is poor. And in the second place, the answer is poor. Suppose I am the respondent and I have no control over the question. What should be my answer if I desire the best possible results in an emotionally charged situation? The answer, "Sure I will go along with you (positive answer so far) (pause), if you will explain or define what I will have to take," is a matter of moving from one level to another in a delicate situation. This is an abbreviated conversation, but, I think it will clarify the idea.

To sum up, extensionalization is the connection between theory and practice and the element which enables us to transform and convert a concept or theory into a workable personal construct. It can be summed up as follows: Does the map represent the territory?

We have described a process that takes place "naturally" in a haphazard manner. By utilizing the construct of hoisting we lift ourselves to a new level and extensionalize about a particular mental theory we have constructed within our "unpure" metaphysical world from a superficial and unconscious inference we have made regarding our empirical world. This process, the epistemological profile, systematized through abstracting and multi-ordinality will enable us to draw more accurate and adequate inferences. Thus, it ultimately enables us to develop valid theories and constructs.

CHAPTER IX

MORE ON EXTENSIONALIZATION: THE FACTORS OF CAUSES, TIME AND SYMPTOMS EMPHASIZED

Occasional Paper Number Five

Extensionalization — Theoretically Considered

Extensionalization has to be a continuous process. It does not give us information we know once and for all. Even at the verifiable stage of extensionalization we run into the problem of time. I used the example of, "how many bricks are in that pile?" In Occasional Paper No. 3, I was trying to illustrate the verifiable extensionalization process, even in this case it is still a tentative designation, tomorrow or the next minute our count may be changed with the liberation of some of the bricks. In terms of 'time', then, our conclusion even at the verifiable stage must be held tentative, with definite 'specification' (See *Knowing and Known* by Arthur Bentley and John Dewey for more on the process of specification as it is used here) and holding constant the elements of time and change. However, this is not a difference which makes a difference except as we use the example to determine crucial future relationships, and except as the verified matter has to do with important matters — e.g., betting of large sums of money and basing the outcome of things of value on whether or not one is correct.

The verifiable stage, for the most part, does not represent the elements of time and change as crucial factors. The stages where the time and change elements are most crucial are: 1) the unverified-verifiable level; and 2) the metaphysically unverified-verifiable category (referred to in Occasional Paper No. 3 as 'unconscious intensional-extensional activity'). I would like to address myself to both of these simultaneously since there is some similarity.

A Case in Point — Causes vs. Symptoms

I once advised a friend of mine, who is divorced, if he should remarry, to marry a younger person. The information I had obtained from my extensionalization process indicated that this was the way to go. It was true for that time. A year later, the process of extensionalization still operating automatically indicated that: (a) it was too much of a theoretical generalization — had allness overtones and had to be held tentative; (b) later information brought to the fore indicated problems that this author had not anticipated which brought about a reversal in opinion. So the element of time made the best suggestion seem as if there were a contradiction — actually there was none. It simply indicated that extensionalization is a process; and that old adage, that truth is relative and contains an integral time factor is relevant. There is no contradiction — what was true a year ago may no longer be true — truth changes with time — so the element of time has to be held constant and extensionalization has to be considered a process and not fixed once and for all; if we are to be reliable in our transactions.

This brings me to another concept — the one of symptoms, in lieu of causes. We must base our conclusions on symptoms, and not 'real causes' because real causes speak to fixation. When we operate within the arena of symptoms, the time factor is implicit. In the case just mentioned above about marriage, for example, all early symptoms indicated that the course of action prescribed should have been followed. But, later symptoms indicated that the course of action would have to be revised and should not be considered a fixed category. Consequently, we must wait for the emergence of new symptoms and for a variety of reasons we can only know what they are with time. Sometimes they don't exist at the time; at other 'times' they just develop 'over time.' By holding time as fundamental we do not confuse symptoms with causes.

This indicates that as we utilize extensionalization in our decision making process, the factors of time and symptoms must be given great stress. It takes time for the symptoms to develop in order to enable us to make an adequate decision. However, we cannot suspend action or allow ourselves to become immobilized — we just must be aware that the truth we have found for the moment is just what it implies, a momentary truth. And, the decisions we make based on one set of symptoms, may change, as other symptoms emerge with time. Sometimes, however, the necessary symptomatic elements are there but we are not psychologically ready to accept what we have extensionalized. Again, time becomes the factor in bringing us around, e.g., a young wife had been telling her older husband that she no longer wanted to be married — that she was undergoing changes and that she felt as if she were missing out on life. She wanted to 'frolic' and have 'fun.' The marriage, she felt, cut down on her freedom; however, on another level she felt that new friends, a new home and more time for a personal life would probably prove the kind of outlet she needed to help her adjust within the marriage. In other words, she felt, the lack of freedom, tiredness from taking care of the kids and the lack of certain tangible things were basic to the frustration being experienced. This appeared plausible until, one night while the two were talking, under somewhat relaxed conditions, she started talking about what she thought of herself at the present time. She said, "I feel ugly, I feel as if I am deteriorating. I feel like an old woman — I ache." Implicit in her remarks, and sometimes explicit, was the idea that the marriage would continue this deterioration. Time enabled her to express more *fully* the symptoms and enabled him to understand more fully. The (so called) 'cause' of her problems was the marriage itself, 'ipso facto,' the additional symptoms indicated. The revelation of the additional symptom threw new light on the matter. Instead of believing that the frustration could be worked out in the marriage and making a decision at a lower multi-ordinal level, the new symptoms raised the level of the transaction. A new element had to be inserted into the equation, not just added, because adding would make it a simple arithmetic affair and defy the concept of the structural more — the new insertion actually moved the decision making to a new dimension where other possibilities had to be considered (like a divorce).

The New Symptoms

The new symptoms indicated that the young wife could only visualize being single; this she was reluctant to admit as a way of finding out whether or not she was missing out on life and no matter what things were provided in marriage in terms of freedom and potential 'things' she would still have a 'feeling' that she was deteriorating. The marriage had begun to be equated with old age, a stopping of life and deterioration regardless of what exercises of freedom provided from within. The first set of symptoms indicated a possibility within the marriage. The second set of symptoms became more overarching and all embracing; and, would eventually nullify lower order action taken within the marriage to cope with the situation. This again illustrates the importance and significance of time and symptoms in extensionalization, i.e., in reaching decisions based upon our check system and personal construct.

Conclusions

The extensionalized symptomatic situation based on the element of time suggested that the action taken had to be raised to a higher level. It indicated that the young wife's overarching theoretical frame had to be dealt with not by just providing answers to concrete lower order symptoms that would have some impact; but, might not provide solutions to concrete lower order symptoms. The appropriate prognosis, in order to alter the situation, is that symptoms of the symptoms had to be dealt with in multiordinal fashion. Continual extensionalizing, time and multiordinality, i.e., symptoms of symptoms determine the proper level of attack. The kind of decision we make in this kind of matter and other similar matters will be determined by a whole variety of factors. Some are: the kind of and amount of confidence we have in ourselves; our own personal adequacy; fears and hopes; our own personal construct about life; what we want out of life; and the kind of life we want to live. The kind of decision to be made in the case above and in the two theoretical extensional areas outlined are usually of the utmost importance, because the level of concern means that the process or the problem permeates almost every aspect of the relationship in some form and will be tested — over and over again. We can look upon it as a long "cold winter" or a chance for growth and development, etc. Our outlook, personal construct will determine what decisions we make and the kind of life we will lead.

Time and symptoms, in addition to making our extensionalization more adequate, enables us to move to more accurate levels of theoretical activity, and move adequately conceptually to the metaphysical unverified verifiable level. This is where our advanced theoretical natural science operates. The physician deals with symptoms and so does the theoretical natural scientist. In the social sciences we try to deal in causes; thus, verbally and actually leading ourselves to dead ends and not realizing that we are. It is, many times, a simple change in words leading to new conceptual outlooks; new social sciences and a 'new' public administration. This brings me to the concept of *science of the process* that will be treated in Occasional Paper No. 6.

CHAPTER X

THE EPISTEMOLOGICAL PROFILE: A NEW DIMENSION

Occasional Paper Number Four

The TWA reservation hostess was talking to her associate about a boy who had left home the day his mother died of cancer — he was in training at the time, at the New York Police Academy. He had seven sisters and a brother. He left New York and went to Chicago the day of her death, without any money. His father had come into the TWA office distraught to purchase a ticket for his son to come home. He had told her this story — and wanted the TWA hostess to add 30¢ to the ticket for bus fare in order that he could go home by bus upon reaching New York.

To all of this, the TWA hostess said, "I do not understand how a person could do such a thing, go away the day his mother died and without any money." She in so many words said, "this is not logical." Her friend then turned to me and asked, "does this make any sense to you?" I said, "no, not in our so-called 'normal' thinking." Our brief dialogue ended at that point. I thought to myself as I left, that many of us are at that level of "transaction" in a process world, still attempting to apply the Aristotelian logical system to understand complex situations in a non-static world. Our strict logic and even the first generation tools and techniques of general semantics do not move entirely beyond the application of logic and rationality to a process situation.

The discovery and development of the epistemological profile within the General Semantics epistemological process allows us to look at the above situation with the epistemological profile microscope.

First of all, we can identify the level of the conversation, the semantic reactor workings, and generalize possibly the way this individual (the hostess) thinks and operates in many situations. The last statement is a higher level abstract inference; but, the risk we venture is not very risky in view of our tool for analysis. The person operates, for the most part, at the second level of the epistemological profile; that is, the level of classifying — Let us call a thing what it is, he either makes sense or he doesn't make sense in logical terms, in other words one is either rational or irrational, or right or wrong, or logical or illogical — with vestiges of the sensing level, i.e., the primitive level of understanding human behavior — a thing is what it is; I am correct because I feel so; there is nothing tentative about what I feel.

Secondly, we realize that in order for people to understand "things" in more than a mere logical sense, they must operate at the postulating level — the level where things are held tentative, i.e., I do not understand all — at this level we leave multiordinality behind. We break out of a vertical system and allow so called "extraneous factors" to come into play vertically and horizontally. We relate to a process, with assumptions that defy logic and admit that there is an area that we do not explain with words or classify. We merely accept the fact that the person was hearing a different thought which may have provided a creative experience that could not be explained in words. Perhaps at that point the son relived his whole life in terms of the police academy and direction. This becomes the "delicate" area of the "twilight zone", perhaps between bitterness and idealism.

Our "classification" and diagnosis of such behavior determines our action and response — if our response is a logical one, we may be the party to the snuffing out of a unifying experience — (that level five experience which transcends all classification) — or if it is diagnosed as man in search of new meaning and significance, our behavior and response may give rise to a creative experience and foster the development of the level five experience. (That experience which brings about a semantic jump, a revelation, a philosophical commitment and unexplained knowing).

Thirdly, the epistemological profile enables us to give a rough interpretation to what is going on (WIGO), to classify our own behavior and that of others, with the knowledge and understanding that we, too, have only limited insight. We have at our disposal a theoretical guide, a process — like orientation, that may stand the test of time and supply confidence and a non-rigid rationale, for taking action in relation to a situation in an automatic fashion — this is where internalization and mastery come into play again.

How many of us operate at the sensing, classifying, relating, postulating and unifying levels without being aware of it? The extra sense of awareness — and "self-consciousness" as Kenneth Boulding writes in his *Meaning of the Twentieth Century* — involves us in a process which goes beyond "normal" understanding and analysis. It is that methodology which, if progressively and profoundly internalized, will relate us to the concept of multi-ordinality and its limitations along with the possibilities for the other General Semantics tools and techniques.

The epistemological profile provides us with a self-corrective and self-reflective mechanism which enables us to take a look at not only our awareness, but our awareness of awareness. In short, our ability to experience and experiment is improved.

This is the activity which moves 'abstracting' from the strict verbal to the non-verbal. It is the process which enables us to go with confidence where mortals in social science have feared to travel, for fear they would be ridiculed as "mystical", unscientific, and "looney". It is where C. Wright Mills was, when he described the power elite and was seriously criticized by Talcott Parsons, Bell Radicals, Liberals, and highbrows, all for seemingly different reasons, which actually fell into a similar category. It is the level of growth which speaks to the creative potential of man. It is where we begin our journey into modern epistemology and move from learning to the knowing; this represents a difference which makes a difference. It is where we "soar" with our overarching theoretical framework or process and revise and revamp without 'verbosity.' It is the process of looking into a process for the purposes of addressing the potentiality of humans; improving self-management; sharpening our search capability; renewing ourselves and community; finding new openings, deciding on new directions; making accurate and adequate decisions, all emerging out of the transacting and transforming process itself.

I postulate, at this time, that the epistemological profile is the first instrument which enables us to deal with that nonverbal process; and, the unifying stage of the profile is the target and the focus.

I, also, postulate and hold tentative the notion that the understanding of the non-verbal process — explained in the paper on extensionalization as the process by which verification was most difficult — can be obtained by re-definition and the development of new concepts. The example which gives me the best insight and "sticks" in my mind is the example of electricity as described by Korzybski on page 50 of his *Manhood of Humanity,* it states "when people began to look at lightning scientifically they used lightning rods and eventually captured lightning and thus gave us our formulation for electricity". In addition, Korzybski states on page 40, "Some of the greatest and most far-reaching scientific discoveries have been nothing else than a few correct definitions, a few just concepts and a few true propositions. . . . Euclid, Newton, Leibnitz — a few correct definitions . . . sometimes by men of merely good sense and fair talent". Korzybski contends that there is a "natural" process, and that process is abstracting, verbal and non-verbal. I infer from this that he means that the "natural" process of abstracting is also the process which takes place without our knowing it in the non-verbal area. Bois contends that the process is not so natural and that Korzybski has oversimplified the process. They are both postulating and we must hold both contentions tentative. However, there is one thing that they both agree on and that is a process is there awaiting discovery and proper conceptualization; and, it is up to us, the third generation General Semanticists, to make this discovery. We can do so by making the proper effort. The proper effort entails the utilizing of the proper methodology and the proper focus. The proper methodology, at this time is the Epistemological Profile, and the proper focus is the unifying stage and the participating level of that profile.

I also postulate, and quite tentatively, that the separation of the verbal and non-verbal worlds is somewhat like all of our other separations. Korzybski said . . .

> "I firmly believe that the consciousness of the difference between these levels of abstractions, i.e., the silent and the verbal are the keys and perhaps the first step for the solution of human problems. . . . If we 'think' verbally, we act as biased observers and project into the silent levels the structure of the language we use . . . when we think *without words,* or in pictures . . . we may discover new concepts and relations on silent levels, and so may produce important theoretical results, in the general search for similarity of structure between the two levels, silent and verbal. Practically all important advances are made that way." (Korzybski, *Manhood of Humanity,* page XVLIII)

There is, in my judgment, not that sharp a separation, one blends into the other, we can, however, be aware of the differences. Even so subscribe to his thesis that one should not superimpose the old verbal language on non-verbal activity, that we should develop forms from the silent world by operating in the silent world. However, this smacks of the old school of phenomenology. While it is desirable, it may not be the way we can operate, at least at this time.

We must recognize, with reference to the silent world, that there is a 'gold mine there'. The key is being aware as to how one relates to the other in some "natural" way. I believe, and this is pending extensionalization, they build, develop and nourish each other in an 'invisible' fashion. Our major task is to make sure our verbal world is in line with modern epistemology. And the tools and techniques of the General Semantics Epistemology that are 'below' the level of the fifth stage and first level (unifying and participating) of the Epistemological profile, if sharpened, will aid us in understanding both the non-verbal and verbal more conceptually.

CHAPTER XI

AN OVERARCHING FRAMEWORK – SCIENCE AND THEORY OF THE PROCESS

Occasional Paper Number Six

The Process

As I went through a week of not being sure of my knowledge and where I was in terms of building my systematic approach to the world of knowing and how we know what we know, I started reading *Knowing and the Known* by Arthur Bentley and John Dewey. I felt as I read it that I would never understand it, and that much of what they were saying was already a part of our social science methodology. And, we were already using the process they were talking about, perhaps not systematically, but talking about it and writing about it. I decided that a systematic use was as important as the inculcation of the Process; hence, systematizing became a key element.

After about three days I began to emerge from my unsteady "state" which could be classified as 'tension,' 'anxiety,' a feeling of not being at one with 'process' and general ineptitude. In other words, an 'uneasy feel.' As the emergence took place I began to better understand the book (especially as I made the concept of systematizing more prominent), I got a feeling for some new concepts. As I thought about the processes we were using in my classes, which were undefined; and as I related to *Teaching as A Subversive Activity* by Neil Postman, I began to think about convergence, systematizing of theories in order that they might enable us to pull things together. I stated in one of my Position Papers that our basic interest was in redefining and immersing ourselves in conceptual activity. I added that a critical problem was that our theories did not hang together in any systematic fashion — did not offer us a frame of reference that would enable us to comprehend, embrace and develop an umbrella for substantive theories that we seem to, at the present time, use in tool box fashion, i.e., in an isolated sense. I also alluded to the fact that we needed an overarching theoretical process which would enable us to become more effective. Based on the postulate that a good practitioner was also a good theoretician — that the two were not separate. Also, that we operated from within a theoretical frame — with a personal construct which had been developed over time. This personal construct gave direction to our decision-making process. So the question was raised, if this be the case then we should make sure that we operate from within a process which speaks to change, to a revamping of old outmoded notions and the theory itself; and also, that we develop a heightened awareness and be committed to the proposition that the internalization of the theoretical process was a key element.

As I thought about these things and read Bentley's *Knowing and the Known* and kept emerging in a process-like fashion from the unsteady states, the key which I had been looking for unfolded. I had said much earlier, in other papers that the 'how' would emerge out of the 'what' — but I knew this would not be sufficient because from the what to the how, a process takes place. Then, how do I describe that process? I decided that making an attempt to describe the process would give us the added dimension, i.e., the systematized process that we were looking for.

Bridgeman, writing an essay in *Life, Language and Law,* edited by Richard W. Taylor, entitled *Error, Quantum Theory, and the Observer,* gave me additional insight into the how of the situation and I paraphrase: in order to understand the submicroscopic process of the quantum world and make what happens there, applicable to our decision-making and creative process; we must concentrate on building a more "scientific" macroscopic world, addressing ourselves to the one significant tool that we have, the language and humankind as a symbol-maker. He also intimated that the so called two worlds verbal and non-verbal — the sub-microscopic and macroscopic are not separate. Looking at them in synthesis was proper. This, to me, was an additional tool for us, again, the *structural more*.

I postulated in Occasional Paper No. 5 that one way of building a systematic approach to the world of knowing was through extensionalization and the developing of a process which emanates somewhat, from the *overarching theoretical framework*.

Overarching Theoretical Framework or Process

The overarching epistemological framework based on the latest findings in modern epistemology automatically gives us our set of values, our process, our frame of reference. We do not have to see poverty to know poverty; we do not have to see killing to know it is inhuman; we do not have to experience exploitation to know that it is bad and is a serious handicap to future progress of humankind. Our overarching theoretical framework based on modern epistemology dictates our set of values, our policies, our objectives, our ways of organizing, our activities, our decisions and, finally, our actions. We follow a course of action dictated by the frame of reference. To construct and chart a course of action for any substantive group of activity becomes a matter of process and method. Whether it be banking, priorities in government, welfare system, education, police matters, economic development, or other matters, our priorities and direction are already determined. The right action is not one of 'conscious' selection; it is a matter of bringing to bear the overarching theoretical frame we live with from day to day. It directs us; so, the question isn't how much we know about a particular subject; but, how well have we developed that epistemological frame of reference and what it is based on, i.e., does it allow us to pursue humanistic goals. This overarching framework is part and parcel of our methodology — another way of saying it is: means and ends connect.

The Science of the Process

The factor which moves and gives expression to the statement, 'the how emerges out of the what' is the *'theory and the science of the process.'* The question becomes how does it emerge out of the what or what ingredients are involved? Our first commitment is to extensionalization; our second commitment is non-separation of the verbal and non-verbal worlds and non-separation of macroscopic, sub-microscopic, and microscopic; the third commitment is to symbolic behavior as the major instrument for creation and one of the keys to better understanding of Bois' epistemic process (for more on this see *Breeds of Men* — Harpers, 1970).

This brings me to the fundamentals which we must by all means hold tentative — and must internalize in order to address ourselves to the creation of the science of the process. The first fundamental is a broad one: we must be aware of how the concepts, and eventually constructs, are linked together in a conceptual pattern, in other words, the concepts and constructs must be examined to determine if they hang together in a system (this will bring us to the concept of convergence). The second fundamental is that we understand the extensionalizing criteria which lead us to know what we know.

For the first, on an ongoing basis, we must insist that the concepts converge before they are made constructs. In a discussion of multi-ordinality, I easily move to a discussion from abstracting, to non-identity, to non-allness, to map vs. territory, to accurate vs. adequate, to differences that make a difference, to self-reflexiveness, to time-binding, the epistemological profile, and the process of the process, etc.

The second, is that we understand the fundamentals in the science of the process itself which automatically take form in the process we are trying to understand. There are two levels:

one has to do with the overarching premise that is all-encompassing. That is, the concepts or methodologies with the premises function from Knowns to Knowings or from named to namings. The known and the named are the events themselves from which 'knowledge' information and understanding of phenomenon is obtained. This is the cosmos we allow it to flow. The whole organism environment complex is our 'oyster.' The knowings and the namings have to do with how we interpret the events — separately and together. The idea is to develop a 'feel' for the overarching framework so that it works automatically in postulation.

Theory of the Process or Method of Inquiry

In our overarching process there are several ingredients we must keep in mind — we begin with the fact that in order to know we must be aware of what we want to know. We want to know the actual event, i.e., the known is the event and what we call it is the named — moving from there we want to know how we know what we know. Well, we know by a process called knowing and naming. This is the overarching abstracting process by which we try to interpret the events on an on-going basis. So we have the known or the event; and, the *knowing* or *naming* which is the *process* of the *process.*

When we rise to the third level, the science of the process we must try to describe — so, we take a stab, within the overarching it manifests itself as follows:

1. The first is the *sign* which *covers all* — we must look for signs which convey to us certain information — this is non-linguistic.

2. The second is signal — the signs symbolically come through some kind of signals — this is the first step beyond the sign.

3. The third is cue which is tied in with signal — it merely gives us an extra nudge. It comes through language.

4. The fourth is the process of characterization — with this process we bring the cues together in some kind of whole. In other words, we hang them together in some kind of system.

5. The fifth is a major step — it is when we start naming and

designating what we are talking about — we say what we think it is.

6. The sixth stage is descriptive — we try to describe it in the best way possible, in order to provide a measure of order.

7. The seventh is specification. Here we distinguish the description from other descriptions in order to make it distinct. We note similarities and differences.

8. The eighth step is definition — in this process we begin to become very conscious of what we do; we refine with hunches, symbols, and anything that comes to us. We move again to sign, cue, characterization, description, specification, in order to elaborate and make the description more scientific, workable and conceptually accurate and adequate.

Of all the steps in the process I consider *cue* the most important. We always receive cues — it is whether or not we are aware or psychologically ready to accept. The example of cue in its best form is illustrated by an incident of which I heard. There was a fellow who could never break an appointment. He was about to marry a girl, about a month before their marriage he was going away and would not return until the eve of their marriage — he had a two o'clock appointment with a close friend, he had made two days before he knew he was leaving. Upon learning this she asked him to break the appointment in order that they might discuss some things. He refused. She was hurt and could not understand why he could not. She decided to postpone the marriage indefinitely in order to extensionalize the situation. She later learned that this was a pattern and would make for difficulties for both of them. The relationship was subsequently terminated. We receive many cues of this type, some important — some not so important. The *cue* will enable us to describe, specify, and subsequently define with a fair amount of accuracy the situation. Thus, enable the decision-making process to move in some kind of 'invisible' '*natural*' order. The time element is important, because, it not only allows us to establish a pattern; but, also allows additional symptoms to arise which may establish the pattern as something that can be easily handled; or, it may give us insight into a deeper pathological problem; emanating from the very base of our philosophical construct, which permeates the very 'fabric' of the relationship. In short, it may not be as isolated as it seems — cue is important to broaden specification and definition. The process — in short: transaction is inquiry of a type in which existing descriptions are accepted as tentative. Specification is the most efficient form of designation at one end of the range, and is followed by three stages of designation, using language as the form of symbolization. Given such a *map of the territory,* the various sorts of human procedures are lumped together under the name of definition. What I am doing, falls under the heading of the process of definition. Therefore, it looks something like this: designation is behavioral, that procedure of naming which comprises the great bulk of linguistic activity. It lies intermediate between earlier perceptual activities of signaling and the later and more intricate specification. Specification opens and ranges by the use of induced descriptions and its specialized activities of symbolizing under the above approach, naming, is seen as a direct form of knowing. Then, in an overarching sense:

1. Transaction-abstracting
2. Named-naming, knowing-known
3. Sign-process
   a. Signal
   b. Designation
      1) cue
      2) description
      3) specification
4. Definition

It is an intimately connected process and the above takes place in that order, and, simultaneously, all cropping up at every stage — one just being more dominant than the other at a particular time. It is a transaction process with the dissecting taking place only for analytic purposes — in a synthetic sense the model is the viewed epistemic process — sub-microscopic process, microscopic-macroscopic, verbal-non-verbal, content-container, and time dictating the dominant factor — the overarching frame of reference is transaction, and postulation in combination in an attempt to describe natural processes taking place in synthesis.

This may be seen as a postulated beginning in trying to understand the natural decision-making process from a holistic standpoint. It is a prelude to action and hopefully moves us to a new conceptual level.

The Importance and Need for an Overarching Theoretical Process

Boulding, in the *Image and Meaning of the Twentieth Century,* has said it; Postman, in *Teaching as a Subversive Activity* has said it; Bois, in the *Art of Awareness, Explorations in Awareness, Breed of Men,* and his new manuscript, *New Directions* has said it; Bridgeman, in *The Way Things Are* has said it; Korzybski, in *Science and Sanity* and *Manhood of Humanity* has said it; Lincoln Barnett, in the *Universe and Dr. Eisenstein* has said it; Pierre Teilhard de Chardin in *How I Believe, The Phenomenon of Man* has said it; Bronowski in *Science and Information* has said it; and, I could go on naming them. But, the person who has put it in perspective for us and, in my judgment, laid the groundwork for the future of Public Administration is Professor Alberta Guerriero Ramos — writing in his *The New Ignorance and the Future of Public Administration in Latin America,* he said this:

> "Of course, a minimum theoretical consensus is an essential requirement of any scientific community, without it, cooperative efforts and a process of theory building cannot take place. . . Such ignorance is not overcome until a basic framework of inquiry is structured consistent with the new historical trends. . . There is the unguessed ignorance of those who do not realize the obsolescence of their intellectual schemes and structures in relation to the new circumstances and try unsuccessfully to marshal them resorting to extrapolations. . . On the other hand there is the self-conscious ignorance, which deserves to be called, in line with the classical expression of Nicholas of Cusa, *learned*

ignorance (octa ignorantia). This is the ignorance we must not be ashamed to recognize as ours at this point in the history of our field. . .
In fact, if we develop thoroughly the idea, we find ourselves tackling the problem of reconceptualization of science and of its practice. . . From this follows, according to Cieszkowski, that the ordinary human action can have a philosophical or theoretical content. . .
If public administration is to be a scientific field, it has to rely on a set of basic assumptions that are the same in Latin America and everywhere. . . The classical thinkers did not face a situation of technological and economic development and interdependence as we have in the present days. . . Today, however, technology has made the world a concrete single system. There is no isolated place in the planet. World problems exist now without solution, unless an effort of institution building is systematically undertaken in planetary scale. . . No national society today can be understood on the basis of its internal processes and conditions alone. Nations are penetrated systems in the sense that the allocation of their resources and values results considerably from their need to cope with pressures from the international environment."

I have quoted from a paper Ramos wrote which is not for citation; I obtained verbal permission by phone, April 17, 1970.

What he has said ties in with the development of what I have referred to as an overarching theoretical framework, which should not only enable us to predict and understand "historical trends" as Ramos puts it; but, also "epistemic trends" as Bois sees it. In this context historical trends lag behind epistemic trends. In order to project ourselves beyond historical trends, the process must not only be global but cosmic; and it must of necessity delve into the possibility of a quantum-like undertaking of what we are all about. And, it must be transactional, with a better understanding of the *known* and the *knowing*; and, all must be permeated with tentativeness and undergirded by consistent postulation.

If we should fail to develop along the lines outlined in Ramos' paper — and Bois' design, we will find ourselves marooned at the stage of feeling inferior to the "natural sciences." Part of our problem in the social sciences is that we have felt inferior to the natural scientist; but, I state categorically that we are not. We can move and soar by subscribing to dimensions that defy logical analysis and macroscopic empirical testing. We should make that semantic jump. Our confidence tempered with postulative action becomes an important ingredient. In short, our methodology has to match our projected model. Moreover, the methodology has to contain a philosophical commitment and direction in order that automatic revision may occur. The day is long since gone when the two are separate — where methodology should be used for good or evil. In the social sciences — unlike the physical sciences, we deal with human values — and this is a difference which makes a difference — as we develop our methodology. This difference separates, to some extent, physical science from social science. And, this emphasis may be one of the missing elements which will move us where we ought and might be. I postulate this.

CHAPTER XII

A DIFFERENCE THAT MAKES A DIFFERENCE A DIFFERENCE: THE ONE MAN THEORY – A RADICAL PERSPECTIVE

Occasional Paper Number Seven

The Public Administration field should be reorganized to attract those people who are non-traditional in their approach. They should be convinced that we not only are concerned about training technically good managers, but managers who go beyond technique and efficiency and confront the world with a social concern.

As my wife and I were sitting one Sunday morning having breakfast with her family, we were talking about how much she was like her mother, at least this is what I was saying. I watched her eyes and volunteered that there was, however, a difference! She then said I hope it is a difference which makes a difference a *difference*. I had used the language before in this fashion but not adding the other dimension. A difference which makes a difference was coined by Wendell Johnson, the General Semanticist, in *People in Quandaries*. I have used it often but never in this fashion. The phrase again, "a difference which makes a difference a *difference*" is implicit in a "difference which makes a difference"; but when we say it two things occur:

1. It is made explicit.
2. We broaden our conceptualization which might make a difference in our findings.

Thus, let me depart here and talk about differences that make a difference a *difference* and see if anything has been expanded by looking at the phrase in this explicit fashion. I will use the phrase in connection with my concept and interpretation of the One Man Theory which I coined recently.

The One Man Theory

I remember when Eugene Talmadge of Georgia died. Black people in the South rejoiced. There was an underlying assumption that things would change. Then his son, Herman, took over the Governorship. Things proceeded similarly to the way they were before. Georgia remained a suppressed and segregated State for Black people.

I remember when Senator Bilbo of Mississippi died. Blacks applauded and celebrated. Then Senator James Eastland took his place — a segregationist of the first order.

Minor changes may have taken place. Time itself produces some, that is, to some extent the structure of the world does (epistemic process). But we have learned, I think, that a system produced those individuals and the system is inherited by others. Those others may have the best of intentions but very little can be done in terms of real, meaningful change. In other words, it is a difference that does not make a difference a *difference*.

The major pitfall in assuming that individuals make a major difference is that it gives us a false focus. When we focus on the system and not the individual, we level our attack in useless places and where it does less good. For example, one of my students wanted to impeach Richard Nixon. This is a laudable act, considering the way I see Nixon's fundamental assumptions, personal construct or epistemological framework, i.e., it provides us with an absolutist and false notion of the world and direction for humankind. Impeaching Nixon would have to be only a beginning. He is a product of the system. Possibly the main dangers in selecting this as a focus are: 1) it is a long drawn-out process that requires limitless energy and organization; 2) we tend to identify what we are doing with major change, when it is not; 3) it may maroon us at levels where we become less effective; 4) we fail to attack the system which gives rise to Nixonites, i.e., we use the system to get rid of Nixon and in those tools and techniques lie assumptions about the world that may not speak to transformation; and 5) the results may not match the energy input. This, however, is one way of attacking problems. It may not, however, be a difference which makes a difference a *difference*.

The One Man Theory holds that those who would like to bring about major changes must adopt first of all a relativistic view rather than an absolutist view. This view must tie our assumptions, frameworks and personal constructs to modern epistemology in a way that enables us to build a process that is in keeping with the process of the world and the cultural and automatic epistemic changes that are taking place. This is the beginning of a difference which makes a difference a *difference*. In other words, we must be sure that we not only have a map of the territory for limited cases, but subscribe to a process level which is biological. It is tied to growth change emergence and transformation. This is not just a "map of the territory," but an assumption that a map is self reflexive. The so-called mapper is a semantic reactor involved in a process that is akin to quantum mechanics and he must, if he uses the map analogy, realize that it is not only inadequate, but is made inaccurate with time, and must substitute abduction for deduction. This is a difference which makes a difference a *difference*.

The One Man Theory also holds that one man can make a difference a *difference* if he levels his attack where it can do the most good. If he sees conflict as the only way, or by the same token, if he sees cooperation as the only way, he has limited himself in terms of impact. But, if we use *multiordinality* as a concept which enables one to see many levels of attack and we choose the most appropriate one for ourselves, one where the energy input is less than the energy output, then this man becomes a difference which makes a difference a *difference*, and one man can make the difference.

Using the epistemological profile to understand personal constructs, assumptions, identification problems, and to predict behavior and situations, is a difference which makes a difference a *difference*. With this attitude and tool, one man can make a difference.

Realizing that there is an inseparable relationship between theory and practice, between theory and action is a difference which makes a difference a *difference*. And, that the kind of theories we construct are a prelude to the kind of action taken; and, that this action, based on modern general semantics epistemology, moves us closer to effective action that is a difference which makes a difference a *difference,* and makes one man a difference.

I postulate here that the ability to program what we know automatically emerges out of the well-defined what. In this case, our well-defined what is the overarching framework. Our decisions relative to the how are based mostly on this framework. Our vehicles for action emerge as we are transformed in this process of self-reflexive mapping of the territory. One profound idea emerging out of the framework may change the course of our life and provide us with direction that will enable us to make an impact on the system wherever we are, and move us from the stage of useless verbosity to a stage of effective action.

One of the strongest elements emerging out of the modern general semantics epistemological framework is one of confidence. Confidence that one has a broad understanding of the world and can link that world to his particular situation. Therein lies significance and meaning, and, if you will, the courage for bold action. The building of the process gives one man power, and it becomes a difference which makes a difference a *difference.*

What gives certain ones courage to face death? It, to some, is knowledge arising out of a well-defined situation. It is the linking up of the processes, one to the other, in a very significant way. Some call it transcendence — transcending one's self. One must determine where he is in the total cosmos and how his action relates to the overall objective, if his objective is defined in terms of something broad, say like the system and changes within that system. However, if his overarching framework is small, then his decision will be small and the possibility of change and impact may be limited — and his decision in a particular instance may not be a difference which makes a difference a *difference,* and the One Man Theory does not hold.

Let me give a personal example, which may to some extent, illustrate my point. I was told at a party that the 'space committee' in the School of Public Administration was contemplating 'liberating' me of my office and giving it to a full professor who was returning after being on leave. I immediately grew incensed. For a while I was marooned at the sensing level of the epistemological profile. Then, I moved to the second stage, classifying, of calling names, silently and openly. In minutes I moved to the relating stage. I felt I knew exactly what I would do if someone would attempt to take my office. I was still, however, puzzled by my strong reaction because space in itself never meant that much to me. Then I got another feeling that I would have to be bodily removed, fired and would be a party to my own dismissal and would even die before I would voluntarily move. I didn't ask myself why, I merely allowed my overarching process which embraces multiordinality, the epistemological profile, and the second generation tools and techniques of modern General Semantics epistemology to take over. The action became a clear one, also the immediate symptoms for my semantic reaction became clearer. The criteria I assumed being used by the committee was counter to my overarching framework and spoke to our archaic social system which I was committed to change. In this case I could see the rank concept as being a part of the old system which needed changing. The criteria being used was the object not the office. At that point I considered dying or being a party to my own dismissal confronting the situation; and that confrontation in this case would be in keeping with my overall orientation to change the system. It would be a broad outlook in a small circumstance on the injustices in the systemic framework which pervades our society and the world. Thus, I could make my contribution at this point, without immobilizing myself. The clearness of this situation arose out of my framework; thus, providing courage, significance and meaning to a seemingly harmless and innocent situation but had great symbolic meaning in terms of change. When we begin to relate the symbolic ordinary situation to the wider implications there is no room for 'copping' out and we do not have to 'impeach' Nixon or wait for a large situation in order to make our impact as one man. It is a difference which makes a difference a *difference*. Thus, our modern epistemological framework and overarching framework as a process is not only an abstract theory but a prelude for action wherever we are.

The transcending of logic can be extended to our system. Whenever one states that we should work within the given frame of reference, we set up logical constrictions. Most of our officials, when talking about student unrest, violence, revolts, rebellion, usually say that it is better and necessary for those participating to do it non-violently and with peaceful dissent. The very same system that the people are fighting to change constricts their actions. This is part and parcel of the language structure that Aristotle handed to us. In order to break the bonds of this constriction, it is necessary for those participating in the demonstration and those who put restrictions on the demonstrators to become translogical in order that they might deal with a framework and premise as well as what the framework and premise embrace. This is a difference which makes a difference a *difference* and gives content to the one man theory.

When one works without direct challenge to the system, the major premise or the process from which things flow, it is a difference without a difference, a change within the structure without coming to grips with the common sense notions of reality. So we must be translogical in our approach. If we are translogical then behavior does not become the issue but the situation and whether or not those notions within the situation can only be changed in extraordinary fashion. Each situation becomes then sociological and if you will epistemological in content. Not right or wrong, not legal or illegal but epistemological in content. Not right or wrong, not legal or illegal but epistemological and translogical.

Working entirely within the system is, many times, a change

without a difference and fatalistic in projection. Take the statement made by Professor of Law at Stanford University, Tony Amsterdam, "After the revolution I will be representing the capitalist," Time Magazine, May 25, 1970, p. 67. He was indicating that he likes to defend the underdog. His statement does not indicate that we can undergo a revolution that speaks to transformation. He is a victim of the system and continues to work within it — logically, consequently he views no real change.

Our target can be institutions and individuals but our bull's-eye must be the system. Two different levels of concern must be launched simultaneously. One rhetorically kept in mind (the system) and attacked in particular situations and the other (institutions) attacked constantly.

Every act personal or general must in some way incorporate implications of change within the system. It is risky and possibly one might be a party to his own dismissal. But, it represents a difference which makes a difference a *difference* and gives the one man theory substance.

The representation I have given thus far builds a case for the 'particular case' model of conflict due to the systemic implications involved. There are limitations to confining oneself to the 'particular case' model of conflict but it can be a useful one. What makes this so? In order to determine the direction we need to see conflict within the multiordinal framework and only as a particular case within the broader overarching process. Let us look at it as a 'particular case.'

Conflict

Conflict theories are alike in their rejection of the order model of contemporary society. They interpret order analysis as the strategy of a ruling group, a reification of their values and motivations, a rationalization for more effective social control. Society is a natural system for the order analyst; for the conflict theorist it is continually contested political struggle between groups with opposing goals and world views. Social problems, therefore, reflect, not the administrative problems of the social system, nor the failure of individuals to perform their system roles as in the order explanation, but the adaptive failure of society to meet changing individual needs.

Contemporary liberalism has been popularly associated with a conflict model of society; actually it is a variant of conservative order theory. Within the model, conflict is translated to mean institutionalized (reconciled) conflict or competition for similar goals within the same system. Conflict as confrontation of opposed groups and values, conflict as a movement toward basic change of goals and social structures is anathema.

A certain egalitarianism is indeed implied in at least two liberal assertions: (1) Black along with other men share a common human nature socializable to the conditions of society; (2) their low position and general inability to compete reflect unequal opportunity and inadequate socialization to whatever is required to succeed within the American system. These asseverations are, in a sense basically opposed to the elitist-conservative argument that the Black has failed to compete because he is naturally different or has voluntarily failed to take full advantage of existing opportunities.

The conservative, however, exaggerates liberal egalitarianism; it is tempered with elitism. Equality is won by conformity to a dominant set of values and behavior. Equality means equal opportunity to achieve the same American values; in other words, equality is gained by losing one's identity and conforming at some level to another demanded by a dominant group. As a leftist, J. Sartre has summarized this liberal view of man, both egalitarian and elitist. What he has termed the "democratic" attitude toward the Jew applies well to the American "liberal" view of the Black.

Thus, the liberal fate of minorities, including Blacks, is basically containment through socialization to dominant values. Supposedly this occurs in a plural society where some differences are maintained. But liberal pluralism like liberal egalitarianism allows differences only within a consensual framework. This applies both to the liberal idea and the sociological description: the plural-democratic society is the present society.

As Sartre rightly observed, the liberal who is himself identified with the establishment, although avowedly the friend of the minority, suspects any sign of militant minority consciousness. He wants the minority to share in American human nature and compete like an individual along with other individuals for the same values.

The liberal solution to the racial question and student revolts follows from the American-dilemma thesis: The belief in the ethical nature and basic legitimacy of American institutions. Amelioration, therefore, becomes exclusively a question of adjustment within the system; it calls for administrative action: How to attack anomie as the imbalance of goals and means. The administrator accepts the goals of his organization and treats all problems as errors in administration, errors which can be rectified without changing the basic framework of the organization. Karl Mannheim has aptly characterized the bureaucratic and administrative approach to social problems. Conflict, if not seen as multiordinal, confines us to one issue and does not allow us to broaden our attack. Our method becomes synonymous with the situation. And, we are blinded to other possibilities. In essence, it is pretty difficult to expand our transaction and conflict case model which maroons us within the institutional framework and leaves the system intact. We rise above the institutional level when our structural methodology is broadened. If we do not do this we follow a line of thinking which misses the crux of the matter and eyes the target; but, not the bull's-eye. It is a difference without a difference.

Those of us involved in the war in Vietnam must realize that this is only one substantive matter. This value attitude will continue in terms of other matters. We must continue to move to new levels of involvement — we must remember that it is not the substance itself but the methodology, process and attitude threading throughout. The war in Vietnam, the racial issue, and attitudes toward education are vehicles which allow us to rise to new levels of involvement. We embrace and cover more — and no matter at what level we are at we must be certain that the new constructs contain universal values and universal concepts — play around or try to hit the target, but be sure we know where the bull's-eye is. It is a difference which makes a difference a *difference* — and makes one man important.

Clarence Darrow said, "I have never met a man I could not like". This is a meaningful statement when you transcend individuals that look at the system. Our epistemological framework dictates the kind of society we perceive. To have one which directs us properly is to first change our focus. We do not necessarily, put the blame on people within the system. We begin with the assumption that the system is at fault — mind you — however, this is only a beginning. If we decide differently we only make "scapegoats" out of the victims of the system — and thus, no change has taken place. The example brought to mind is this: A change without a difference would be Blacks taking over the existing institutions without addressing themselves to the revamping of the system. Black suppression is no better than white. Only the color can change. So we must opt for transformation among blacks, the young and the system. It is essential for survival.

When groups push for change whether it be through violent or peaceful means, the meeting of same with violent methods might enable one regime to displace another but it does not make for change. If the conflict is met with peace it is an appeal to the best instincts in man. It is impossible for the violent and the peaceful to confront each other without a transaction taking place. The transaction is not a reaction, it is a coming together in conflict where both sides emerge different. There are no winners, no losers, no one is overthrown, the system is confronted and conflict is institutionalized. There are no victims — property may be destroyed but human life is preserved. The ends and the means cannot be separated. Understanding the situation transforms a destructive situation into peaceful ends. This is a difference which makes a difference a *difference*. One man can make the difference.

We must move from the stage of saying what "man is all

be doing and where I am. The critical question is what do I do to change the system? How do I transact with a violent and conflict situation? Herein lies the hope. The one *man* theory. Enough action from those who "really" care and begin to see epistemologically their individual roles without generalizing rhetorically in terms of "policy questions" and what "they" ought to do, can bring about the historical change which is being helped already by the epistemic change, quantum in nature.

Individuals operating with a moral philosophy and with the idea that they will personally be a party to their own dismissal in personal situations that have systemic implications can be a difference which makes a difference a *difference*. This gives substance to the one man theory and moves out of the realm of pessimism.

Our major concern is how do we develop methodolgy enabling us to become a difference which makes a difference a *difference*, and makes the one man theory a reality. The answer is, to some extent, in our structural assumptions about what we are all about. The answer, also to a certain extent is internalizing the methodologies in the General Semantics formulation in a systematic and process-like fashion and seeing how certain concepts hang together as in this paper, i.e., a difference which makes a difference a *difference* and the one man theory. They give rise to each other. Means will be discussed in the next occasional paper.

CHAPTER XIII

TOWARD A UNIFIED THEORY: A THEORETICAL PROCESS

Occasional Paper Number Eight

I. *Science of the Process*

I have a theory that we can begin with the overarching theoretical frame of reference as philosophy; include within that frame a process: the formative tendency of the world, what is going on (WIGO), the science of the process (study), the theory of the process (mechanism), and the process. This becomes our epistemological process. We insert the language dimension to modern epistemology as a vehicle, a method, or a technique, if you will. All of this is abduction, not deduction. The difference is that the former is held tentative, the latter is not.

We move within our frames from this 'procedural process region' to the 'substantive procedural process' region. Here we include: abstracting as a process (identification), multi-ordinality, self-reflexiveness, non-elementalism, the epistemological profile, and structural more. Then we move to the extensionalizing area, (technique, tool or methodological level), at this level all I have said above is put to use through extensionalization. This is a way of checking out, revising, and/or making our abductions more contemporary. We use, here, as a base or method of inquiry the science of the process and include, the theory of the process, self-reflexiveness, multi-ordinality, holding constant the process of abstracting, non-identity and non-allness, time binding, the map of the territory, and differences that make a difference a *difference*. We find an active use for the epistemological profile and extend to the devices, viz., indexing, dating, hyphens, etc., quotes and plurals as methods of empirically testing on an on-going, self-corrective and automatic basis the overarching frame of reference and its contents. By reaching out to what is going on (WIGO) and referring back to the frame of reference, our objective is to have an impact on our cortex-thalamic process, the semantic reactor transactive, and thus the delayed movement which produces better self-management and an integrated response which is in keeping with the cortical frame of reference.

As you can see I have not set up a stratigraphic process; but, a unitary process which speaks to a systemic framework. It is self-correcting, self-building, and produces 'particular case situations or constructs', for example, hoisting, vehicles, and growth from a creative standpoint. Moreover, enables us to utilize those particular case situations or constructs in a systematic fashion that are already devised by others, e.g., the law of the situation, span of control, structural more, strategic factor; these can be, usually considered substitutes, results, or by-products depending upon how one perceives the systematic framework. The perceiving is not a matter of 'viewing,' it is a matter of 'feeling' a total process that one lives by. The habitual use of the process is the secret. It eventually penetrates, from the cortical to our nervous system by the use of the extensionalizing process. The extensionalizing process is the linking element which operates in a circular fashion. In order to develop, we then must know something about the matters I have discussed above. This knowing about the process does not provide us with the answer to self-management and effectiveness. It is internalizing by habitual use, the total process. In order to move to a more practical level I will first talk about the knowing. That is, in simpler language: describe what can, might, and may be, and how it may be accomplished. This is the promise of man.

II. *The Overarching Theoretical Process — What can be the Organism-as-a-Whole Approach?*

The organism-as-a-whole approach is fundamental to our

new orientation, symbolism, conflict, change and proper action. All possible characteristics in this world are due to structure, and can be expressed in terms of structure, relations, and multi-dimensional order. This consideration necessitates a non-elementalistic theory of meanings in accordance with the structure of the world and our nervous system; therefore, the organism as a whole cannot and should not be structurally separated from its environment; and so the terms should be enlarged to cover, by implication, the environment and culture. Managing of conflict, managing of self-guided awareness, a deeper understanding, decision-making, and effectiveness, are the end results.

The irony of man's quest for reality is that as nature is stripped of its disguises, as order emerges from chaos and unity from diversity, as concepts merge and fundamental laws assume increasingly simpler forms, the evolving picture becomes more remote from experience — far stranger, and less recognizable.

All highroads of the intellect, all byways of theory and conjecture lead ultimately to a depth that human ingenuity may never span. For man is enchained by the very condition of his being, his finiteness and involvement in nature. The farther he extends his horizons, the more vividly he recognizes the fact that, as the physicist Niels Bohr puts it, "we are both spectators and actors in the great drama of existence." Man is thus his own greatest mystery. He does not understand the vast veiled universe into which he has been cast for the reason that he does not understand himself.

My purpose is to build a systematic way of connecting and synthesizing many concepts, so that we can move from learning to knowing and to action on an automatic basis. We move automatically with this assumption from the mechanical to the biological model which is more in tune with an overarching frame of reference referred to as a process. It is a difference which makes a difference a *difference* and with it one man can make a difference and a greater impact by making a minor basic change in his frame of reference. However, there is a problem, it is the one Einstein encountered. He wanted to unite the laws of gravitation and the laws of electromagnetism within one basic superstructure of universal law. In the same way that relativity reduced gravitational force to a geometrical property of the space-time continuum. He wanted a Unified Field Theory. "The idea that there are two structures of space independent of each other, the metric-gravitational and the electromagnetic," Einstein observed, "is intolerable to the theoretical spirit." Yet despite all his efforts he could not incorporate electromagnetic field laws into General Relativity. After thirty-three years of exploring endless gambits of manthematical logic he went far toward achieving his purpose. One may ask if he proved that electromagnetic and gravitational force are physically the "same thing." It would be no more accurate to make such a statement than to assert that steam, ice, and water are the "same thing" — though all are manifestations of the same substance. What his Unified Field Theory undertakes is to show gravitation and electromagnetic force are not independent of each other — that they are in very real physical sense inseparable ("Dr. Einstein and the Universe") — but he was not able to combine them. It is a prelude to difference and hopefully better action.

III. *Theory of the Epistemological Process*

A. *Time-Binding*

The two facts which have to be dealt with first, are the two which have most retarded human progress: (1) there has never been a true definition of man nor a just conception of his role in the curious drama of the world; in consequence of which there has never been a proper principle or starting point for a science of humanity. It has never been realized that man is a being of a dimension or type different from that of animals and the characteristic nature of man has not been understood; (2) man has always been regarded either as an animal or as a supernatural phenomenon. The facts are that man is not *supernatural* but is literally a part of nature and that human beings are not animals. We have seen that the animals are truly characterized by their autonomous mobility — their space-binding capacity — animals are space binders. We have seen that human beings are characterized by their creative power, by the power to make the past live in the present and the present for the future, by their capacity to bind time — human beings are time-binders. These concepts are basic and impersonal; arrived at automatically, they are mathematically correct.

It does not matter at all *how* the first man, the first time-binder, was produced; the fact remains that he was somewhere, somehow produced. To know anything that is today of fundamental interest about man, we have to analyze man in three capacities; namely, his chemistry, his activities in space, and especially his activities in time; whereas in the study of animals we have to consider only one factor; their activities in space. (Alfred Korzybski, *Manhood of Humanity,* pp. 66-67.) This ties in with what man's life is all about and dictates an approach: Man's concern even despair, over the worthwhileness of life as a spiritual distress may not be a mental disease. A proper diagnosis must be made in order to pull one through the existential crisis of growth and development. It is not the reconciliation of the conflicting id, ego, superego or to promote adjustment, but consists in fulfilling a meaning, actualizing value and fulfilling a goal. The vertical separation of man and animal provides us with the answer. It is based on the theory of time binding.

B. *Semantic Jump*
What Part Does Semantic Jump Play?

When our deep feelings are involved, the face of our world undergoes a significant transformation. The change in our outlook and personal reactions that takes place is what we call a semantic jump. It is a dimensional step.

The acquisition of a new skill, or any change in our self-moving activities — whether it be relaxation, the practice of sensory awareness, the sudden realization of how it feels to create, or a sudden insight may release a grip and give us a freedom of action that we never dreamed possible before.

The prospect of a bright future is a stimulant that rejuvenates — as the anticipation of a defeat saps our energies, dulls our minds, and spreads gloom all through the world in which we live. (J. Samuel Bois, *Art of Awareness,* p. 108.) This may bring about a dimensional more — referred to as a semantic jump. It is a theoretical part of the modern General Semantics process. It aids us in developing a direction and recognizing what is happening as we delve into the process.

C. *Symbolic Thought*
Symbolic Thought Is Another Part of the Theory.

When Einstein developed his general theory of relativity he went back to Riemann's geometry which had been created long before but which Riemann regarded only as a mere logical possibility, it was symbolism. But he was convinced that we were in need of such possibilities in order to be prepared for the description of actual facts. We need full freedom in the construction of the various forms of symbolism, and construct in order to provide physical thought with intellectual instruments. While we cannot anticipate the facts, we can make provision for the intellectual interpretation of the facts through the power of symbolic thought. (Ernest Cassirer, *An Essay on Man,* p. 218) In addition, it has its roots in time-binding. It enables us to connect the past with the present and the future.

Man's conquest of the world undoubtedly rests on the supreme development of his brain which allows him to synthesize delay and modify his reactions by the interpolation of *symbols* in the gaps and confusions of direct experience, and by means of verbal signs to add the experiences of other people to his own. (Susanne K. Langer, *Philosophy in a New Key,* pp. 35-6.)

The symbolic thought can be developed at any time and should be; it awaits the future and provides a proper dimension to our theory of the process.

D. *The Epistemological Process in Action*
What do We Mean by the Epistemological Process in Action?

At this juncture we move into a description of what actually takes place. This too is a part of the theory, or better still, direction. We address at this point specific elements regarding our nervous system: The nerve impulses move slowly to the cortical region. In the case of a stimulus, out goes a response, single and immediate using one deeply canalized thalamic path. The cortex finds out about the response later — all one can do at that time is rationalize, which is also a cortical function, and 'wish I hadn't done it.' The delay allows what we know to act on what we do. The process of abstracting does not come in at all because it remains cortical; and unless we get the delayed reaction on the thalamic level, the knowledge does not come into play or into action. We must, in addition to abstracting symbols, develop a non-elementalistic language which has thalamic components, i.e., the territory must match the map or the symbolism. This brings us to the consciousness of abstracting, realization of levels, and order of evaluation. We may know a great deal but that does not discipline our actions on the living thalamic level. Hence, we must learn the principles of knowing so we can have definite methods of cortical-thalamic integration. Only then can we learn in higher order abstractions and actually get down thalamically to discipline and bring *order* into transaction. Mainly it is the training in extensionalization from general to specific — from higher abstractions to lower abstractions habitually. High-order abstractions are extremely important. If we are able to move from our overarching frame of reference — which is a process and tentative, high level abstracting, a generalization to specific low level abstracting, and specific situations on an extensionalized basis — we begin to train ourselves in cortical-thalamic, semantic reactor-transaction integrative processes. The high level epistemological process no longer becomes an *ought* but a *can* — it is a process.

Cortical-thalamic ties in with the one-man theory. (Williams

— Occasional paper # 7.) The integration speaks to symbolic reaction rather than signal. How do we began to internalize the time-delayed reaction? How do we teach delayed reaction, extensionalization, and the epistemological profile? The critical question is should the cortical thinking be in line with the thalamic first i.e., should there be a considerable effort to change the thalamus by identifying what is actually going on? Or should I merely concentrate on what I want to take place without reference to understanding the thalamus? Harry Weinberg, *Levels of Knowing and Existence,* emphasizes the latter, so does Frankle, and Bois with his profile. In the former case, we may become marooned at the level of understanding without 'speaking' to change or implementation of that understanding. We see this in persons who understand and can give you an analysis of their mental condition, but cannot move from that stage. No behavioral changes take place, it is just the understanding of a 'sick' situation. So, there is no change, just a description of what is and what ought, but not what may, might and can be. The latter case receives emphasis because it automatically embraces the former case. Our starting point determines the effectiveness of our action. In other words, the cortical-thalamus order makes for a more 'workable' container-content formulation. The reverse order thalamus-cortical provides a less workable container-content formulation. The contention is: The macroscopic provides more to work with than the sub-macroscopic does.

IV. *The Language Dimension of the Epistemological Process*

Treading its way through all communication approaches is General Semantics. Here is the relation between words as symbols and the real world. Words are presumed to be the ultimate stuff of which ideas and attitudes are made. (Norman Powell, *Personnel Administration in Government,* p. 426.) The quest for clarity in ideas and attitudes is primarily a striving for better application of the language.

Because language pervades all aspects of administration, much attention has been given to it in recent years. (Charles Redfield, *Communication in Management,* p. 12.) Most of the inquiries into language, thought, and behavior would largely have remained hidden, indeed, would largely have remained isolated from each other — had it not been for a body of theory which was the direct inspiration of most of the popular educators and writers, who from 1939 on, have made general semantics a familiar term in the United States. This popularization came about simply because of the recognition that all human beings have to elaborate, react to, think, and feel about events, words, and symbols in their environment. It was discovered that there is a sharp contrast between evaluative habits, common in science and technology, where progress has been rapid, and those common in other areas such as philosophy, ethics, and politics, in which confusion has been rife and progress has appeared impossible.

It is important to remember that the main concern is language, not as an isolated phenomenon, but rather as language in action, in the full context of the nonverbalized events which are its setting. Consequently, this chapter is devoted to the study of the relationship between language, thought, and behavior. The basic assumption is that widespread cooperation through the use of language is the fundamental mechanism to organizational survival.

Behavior is a function of the words used. More often than not, thoughts do not select the words used, at particular points in our life. Words, to some extent, determine the thoughts. It can be said with some assurance that language develops out of social conditions and, in turn, influences behavior. (Weller Embler, et al., *Language, Meaning and Maturity,* p. 127.) Thus, General Semantics may be considered of fundamental importance in the science of man. In the social sciences, the neuro-linguistic factors of human behavior are assuming an ever greater importance. There is strong emphasis that both the selecting and the organizing patterns bear a definite relation to the structure of language and to linguistic habits. (Anatol Rapoport, *Language, Meaning and Maturity,* p. 7.)

The task is to analyze and work with the structure of language and to relate that structure to human behavior as well as we can. It is a program to retrain human nervous systems and to transfer thought and action from that of the Aristotelian camp to that of the non-Aristotelian. It is based on the premise that in our human reactions, speech, in general, is not an inborn characteristic, but what special language of what special structure of language we acquire is due to environment and copying. Although it is often the result of unconscious and unintentional activity, copying from a system which puts issues into two camps, day or night, black or white, hot or cold, is not indicative of flexibility. Flexibility is needed and requires a language that corresponds to the 'nature' of man — thus the non-Aristotelian system; First Generation General semantics is based upon this system. (Alfred Korzybski, *Science and Sanity* and *Modern General Semantics Epistemology,* p. 19.)

Today, from childhood on, words and language are first inculcated and the facts that they represent come next, in value. By Modern Epistemological methods, we train in a different order; (Alfred Korzybski, *Science and Sanity,* p. XXXIII and J. Samuel Bois, *Art of Awareness.*) The whole passage from the Aristotelian to non-Aristotelian depends on a change of attitude from intension to extension, from macroscopic and microscopic to sub-microscopic orientation, from subject-predicate to relational evaluation. This orientation suggests organism-as-a-whole principles which are fundamental to non-elementalistic and new concentral thinking. (Korzybski, p. 12).

There are certain summary statements to be made about these levels of abstraction: (1) one level is not the same as any other level; (2) the lower the level of abstraction, the more detailed, dynamic, and process-like reality appears to be; (3) abstractions on all of these levels are unspeakable. They can be spoken about, but they can never be completely transformed into words.

The crucial point to be considered is the relationship between language and reality, between words and 'not' words. Except as we understand this relationship, we run the great risk of straining the delicate connection between words and facts.

There must be an awareness that a fact occurs but once. This is a way of stating that no two things are exactly alike and that no one thing remains exactly the same. It is a way of repressing the process character of reality. It is this lack of correspondence that makes for difficulty. Although facts change, they do not change so utterly or so suddenly as to leave us dumb with surprise. True, there are times when change takes us unaware; this is the basis of comedy and tragedy. But, as long as we remain responsive to the fact of change itself, the ever-changing facts are not, as a rule, unnerving. The language dimension of the epistemological process provides us with a tool for delving more deeply into the modern epistemological process and moving toward a set of values and a philosophy.

V. *The Developing of Philosophy and Values*

Within the Overarching Framework

General semantics epistemology has stood the test of time since 1933 when Korzybski pulled the first formulation together, the notions have been reorganized and revised — self correctively and automatically. The revising mechanism internalized is the formulation itself. The converging lines of the various methodologies provide the mechanics for revision. For example, extensionalization is automatically in process. It touches multi-ordinality, the devices, etc., dates, hyphens, etc. and the epistemological profile. Multiordinality as a methodology touches the other processes and so on. It is virtually impossible to use one methodology without it in some way 'bumping' into another on the non-verbal level, mostly, and verbal level. Therein lies one of the keys to the revamping of all notions on an on-going basis. Another is terminology which is necessarily tied in with a philosophical direction.

Korzybski played with such terms as humanology, human engineering, theory of evaluation, and found them all unsatisfactory. Eventually he 'opted' for General Semantics — Arthur Bentley along with John Dewey, (*Knowing and the Known*), agreed — both had serious doubts as to the appropriateness of the term.

In a special paper written by Dr. J. Samuel Bois entitled "General Semantics and the Growth Centers" (June, 1970), the status of General Semantics was summed up. He attempts to put the terminological problems to rest. The essence of his statement was that General Semantics has moved from the original conception as defined by Alfred Korzybski in *Science and Sanity* in 1933. In 1933, in that document, Korzybski talked about a theory of evaluation based on the process of abstracting. Today Bois is contending that is more than that. By utilizing Korzybski's concept of timebinding we find that we have moved from a theory of mere evaluation to a broad epistemology advocated as a trans-intellectual and translogical process; which does not deny the importance of the process of abstracting, or the nonverbal and verbal distinctions. It goes to the 'heart' of values, purposes, attitudes, awareness, and an overarching framework which enables one to practice effective self-management and become philosophically aware as well as structurally competent.

The history of the movement shows that Bentley in writing about *Kinetic Inquiry,* Dewey writing about *Theory of Inquiry* and Korzybski about the *Theory of Time Binding* had a terminological problem. They all were talking about a quest and search for meaning with an epistemological base. While they differed in terms of 'naming' they shared a commonality with reference to a general system of knowing. Bois taking his cue from Michael Foucault, *Les Mots et les Choses, une Archeologie des Sciences des Humanes* (translated it means: *Words and Things, An Archeology of the Sciences Of Man,* which appeared in English in 1971 as a Pantheon book entitled, *The Order of Things*), says that we ought to call the broader scope built on General Semantics, Modern Epistemology and discard the label General Semantics. I agree up to a point with my teacher and the leading theoretician in the field and second generation General Semanticist that we ought to use modern epistemology, but I humbly disagree with the discarding of the term General Semantics. In order to be effective time-binders we must, in my judgment, recognize and blend the past with the present and the future, even terminologically. Therefore, it is my hope that we will follow the pattern developed in my papers of referring to this general system of knowing, feeling, and becoming which constitutes the dynamic epistemic background of our structural unconscious (Bois, *The Art of Awareness*) as modern General Semantics Epistemology. To distinguish the levels of development, first, second, and hopefully third generation General Semantics Epistemology, to me, enables us to move in a time-binding fashion. The important and significant decision is that we accept modern epistemology and move in that direction.

The modern General Semantics Epistemological approach broadens our approach. It states: Because of complexity, etc. and other things, men, each one personally, must develop a way of assimilating information and dealings with the world. That way ought to be in keeping with a direction which speaks to the value of progress, survival, and living of humankind. It ought to be a methodology, simple enough to be internalized theologically and, multi-dimensional in function. It should take care of the generalized as well as many of the special cases, not all, but many.

Making it possible for a broader understanding is critical. Power, leadership, progress, survival, living, ordering complexity and effective action are by-products of this understanding. Coupled with this understanding or even part and parcel is a philosophical outlook or a philosophy of General Semantics Epistemology (See Jay Morris, etc., June, 1970, p. 213.)

Some types of philosophies are in harmony with the principles and applications of general semantics, others are untenable and in conflict with the basic formulations. These must be strongly condemned by general semanticists on a higher level of abstraction.

By philosophy we should mean nothing less than one's total concern with the human condition and what we do about it; we mean, our vision of the nature and destiny of man and the universe in which he lives; search for meaning; the meaning and values of human existence; and the answers we give to such questions as "Who am I?," "What am I doing here?," "Where am I going?" or "What am I?" and "Where am I?".

Every human being capable of conceptual thought has some kind of answer, however vague or inarticulate it may be, to these questions. Some of the answers we give to these questions are compatible with the principles of modern General Semantics Epistemology, while others must be ruled out as destructive to effective time-binding.

General Semantics has to effect a revision of the basic uncritical assumptions of individuals, especially those assumptions concerning the nature and destiny of man and the universe. We must concentrate on areas of human behavior that first generation General Semanticists have not reached.

General Semantics must not become a kind of intellectual tidbit with which to 'mouth' terms. Many of us know "all about" semantic reactions and multiordinality. We can go up and down the abstraction ladder, and knowingly assure ourselves that the map is not the territory, the word is not the thing. At the same time, however, we appear to be quite comfortable with our old philosophical maps. We talk modern General Semantics Epistemology, but General Semantics has never quite got under our 'skins'; the implications have failed to become part and parcel of our philosophical outlook.

In a very real sense modern general semanticists are revolutionists; advocating the overthrow of institutionalized dogmas and absolutes; and laying a foundation for a Science of Man.

Fundamental to a philosophy for general semanticists is Korzybski's definition of man. Out of this definition general semantics was born. What is man? This is the basic question underlying every philosophical outlook. When Korzybski, in his *Manhood of Humanity* defined man as a "time-binder" — a class of life possessed of the unique capacity to capitalize on the achievements of the past — he rejected as a basis for an understanding of the nature of man two other concepts that are still flourishing in our culture: (1) the zoological concept, which maintains that man is nothing but an animal different from other animals only in degree; and (2) the mythological concept, which asserts that man is a fallen angel, half animal and half something called "divine" — a curiosity of the natural and the supernatural, possessed of a perishable body and an immortal soul. Korzybski labeled these concepts as primitive methods of evaluation.

Fundamental, also, is Bois' Epistemological profile which speaks to 'breeds of men' and makes a distinction between those who speak to 'survival' and those who speak to 'living' and moving humankind forward. (See *Breeds of Men,* and *Art of Awareness,* and his new manuscript which is still in the making — referred to as a philosophical direction for humankind based on modern epistemology and general semantics.)

Fundamental, also, is what I have referred to in my writings as the overarching framework or process. It is summed up best by Bois in his new manuscript: *"To Know in Order to Feel More Deeply, To Feel in Order to Know More".* (Chapter 3 — "Our Place in the On-Going Cosmos".)

I postulate that the revising and decision in situations can arise from the very highest level consistent with a value system based on findings in modern epistemology, the nature of man and where man ought and might be. The major question to be raised regarding the revisions and decisions is: Does it conflict with the very philosophy of the overarching theory, the General Semantics epistemological process and the epistemological profile which orders the functioning and structure of the process.

VI. *Constructs and Particular Cases*

The 'natural' process, as I see it now, is for us to subscribe to the overarching frame of reference or process which emanates from the epistemic world, formative tendency of the world, our relationship to the cosmos and the construct of modern epistemology, in order to keep our overarching frame of reference up to date. This becomes an internalized attitude enabling us to build vehicles for action. Taking for granted that we have already internalized the first generation tools and techniques of modern General Semantics epistemology, i.e., time-binding, multi-ordinality, self-reflectiveness, the indexes, abstracting processes, and so forth, these are necessary tools and techniques for beginning, we keep the process going by staying in touch with modern General Semantics epistemology, and we let our vehicles, strategies and tactics in each situation emerge from the total process. The process is essential for understanding and the implementation of the various situational and middle range theories e.g., law of the situation, span of control, the strategic factor, incrementalism, conflict, cooperation, X theory, Y theory, self-actualizing theory, and logo-therapy. All of these become special cases within the modern General Semantics epistemological process. The developing of which requires an on-going search, serious commitment, continuous study and constant practice. This is not an end, it is a beginning.

From this process flows our science of the process and within the process, theorems, doctrines, postulates, and strategies are vehicles for action and understanding of what is going on (WIGO). It is a circular type spiral.

VII. *In Summary — the Formulation*

The process I have been describing is summed up in the illustration below:

Toward a Unified Theory will be continued in the next paper. I will concentrate on implementation of the theoretical aspects of the General Semantics modern epistemological framework.

IN SUMMARY — THE FORMULATION

CIRCULAR PROCESS-EXTENSIONALIZATION

CIRCULAR PROCESS EXTENSIONALIZATION

Science of The Process

(THE FORMATIVE TENDENCY OF THE WORLD)
WIGO.

OVERARCHING FRAME OF REFERENCE

EPISTEMIC — EPISTEMIC

Historical — THE THEORY OF THE EPISTEMOLOGICAL PROCESS — Historical

Methodology — THE LANGUAGE DIMENSION OF THE EPISTEMOLOGICAL PROCESS — Methodology

General Semantics

Infer 1	Emergence	PHILOSOPHY & VALUES	Infer 4
Infer 2	Emergence	THEORIES & OLOGIES	Infer 3
Infer 3	Emergence	THEORY OF SOCIAL CONFLICT AND CHANGE AND GROWTH	Infer 2
Infer 4	Emergence	CONSTRUCTS	Infer 1

1. Systemic-Institutionlist
2. Logo-Therapy
3. Constructive Alternativism
4. The one-man theory
5. Personal construct theory
6. Postulates and cases

Growth — Hoisting

Vehicles

Law of the situation — Strategic Factor

WIGO — OBSERVATION

CHAPTER XIV

TOWARD A UNIFIED THEORY: APPLICATION OF THE PROCESS

Occasional Paper Number Nine

I. *Backdrop to the Extensionalized Process*

By backdrop I mean the transition between the overarching theoretical process and methods of extensionalization. The backdrop becomes the semi-theoretical frame of reference connecting the theory and the practice, the what and the how, the metaphysical and the empirical. The references above are analytical, in actuality they are synthetic or synthesized and should not be reified. Reification (making real) of the analytical process as if it were synthetic creates a distorted view of (WIGO) what is going on (The event). By the use of multiordinality we consider the analytic process the container and the synthetic process, the contents. We then have a unitary process with horizontal abstracting in action. This can provide a measure of order.

A. *Multiordinality*

Multiordinality deals with orders of abstraction. A word is multiordinal when, without any change in its dictionary meaning, it is used in the same sentence — or the same context — to refer to different orders of abstraction. Multiordinality belongs to the vertical and horizontal aspects of our thinking, feeling, reacting, and transacting.

When we move to the level of reacting and transacting as a semantic-reactor we must approach multi-ordinality from the standpoint of container and content. Let us look at it from the standpoint of what a fact is and how multiordinality enables us to move to a new level of understanding. The example: "I love my wife." This is a fact, but I have just bawled her out, perhaps cursed or even beaten her; and this too, is a fact. Does it cancel out the first fact? If we take the two facts as belonging to the same level of abstraction, it does: loving and cursing her stand in opposition. In strict logic, I cannot claim to love her if I curse her at the same time.

This strict logic, however, does not always correspond to what is actually happening. I may justly claim that I still love her in spite of the fact that I am cursing her. And she may resent the bad treatment she receives and love me at the same time. Shall we account for the apparent contradiction by some complicated psychological theory about the ambivalence of feelings?

We could say that love and hate may co-exist in myself and in my wife at the same time, strange as it may seem; but we don't have to accept this theory as the only theory. The multiordinal formulation is much more simple.

The fact that I love my wife is at a higher order of objective abstraction than the fact that I am actually fighting with her. The two facts don't contradict each other, they are superimposed on each other. The higher-order fact is a broader objective reality that encompasses a multitude of lower-order facts of which the present fighting is only one, lost among all the rest. One fact is the container: "I love my wife". The other is the content: "I am abusive". Multiordinality is a methodical formulation that can apply to any science, for almost every ambiguous explanation that is created in a particular science and, for almost every ambiguous case — as is done in psychology with the theory of ambivalence of love and hate.

If we realize that a characteristic of multiordinal terms is that they can be both containers and contents we quickly realize that these terms are legion. (See J. Samuel Bois, *The Art of Awareness,* pp. 92-3.)

A key to a more adequate understanding of self-reflexiveness is afforded by Korzybski's notion of multiordinality, and as such they have no general meaning. What a multiordinal word "means" is determined by the level of abstraction on which it is used. (Wendell Johnson, *People in Quandaries,* pp. 155, 157-8.)

Examples of multiordinality may be found in abundance, once we begin to look for them, and the disregard of multiordinality may be observed in most cases of personality maladjustment. Let us select an instance, "*Never* and *always* are two words one should always remember *never* to use." In other words, "Always," "Never say never." These are self-contradictory, until we recognize that in each case the "same" word is used on different levels of abstraction. It is in effect a statement about a statement. One can move from one level to another without contradicting himself. It is the multiordinal character of the process of abstracting. In short we can say never when we are talking about never, we can say always when we are talking about always. (W. Johnson, *People in Quandaries,* pp. 157-8.)

A very concrete example of this process in operation was when the Mexican-Americans (Chicanos) sat in on the Los Angeles Board of Education to obtain the re-hiring of Sal Castro. They accomplished this. Then, a group of so-called arch-conservatives sat in on the Board to protest sit-ins. Some people thought they were being contradictory. Actually if you evaluate this in terms of multiordinality we find that since the latter group was sitting in to stop sit-ins they were not in contradiction. In pure logic it would be a contradiction, but when we evaluate it in terms of orders of abstraction (translogically) we find the two activities to be of different orders vertically and at different levels. Moralizing as to whether it should or should not be done in this manner is itself another level and so on.

B. *Concepts vs. Constructs*

We now move to another backdrop area, the psychology of personal constructs all of which may not be communicable, and to that which is ordinarily called intellectual or cognitive. It is applied to that which is commonly called emotional or affective and to that which has to do with action.

While the psychology of personal constructs is concerned with personal constructs all of which may not be communicable, and hence is not really what some would call intellectualized theory, it is important that it be itself communicated and that it be intellectually comprehensible. Here we distinguish between the personal constructs about which the theory is concerned and the concepts which constitute the approach of the theory itself.

If one attempts to translate the *construct* into the more familiar term "concept," he may find some confusion. Our *construct* involves abstraction — in that sense the construct bears a resemblance to the traditional usage of "concept." (George A. Kelly, *A Theory of Personality,* pp. 69-70, 130.)

The point I am trying to make is that we move from concept to construct. The construct becomes our personal philosophic commitment. It is a way of knowing and a backdrop process for extensionalizing. (See occ. paper #5 on Extensionalization — Williams).

C. *The Epistemological Profile*

We move now to the epistemological profile the "newest" backdrop frame — it is a prelude to action. The concepts within the profile are not limited to a particular stage; most of the time they are a mixture of thinking models that belong to different epochs in the history of Western Man. If we would represent in a bar diagram the relative amounts of various types of thinking that enter into a particular concept, we would have Bois' epistemological profile giving us a picture of the spreads and peaks of our semantic reaction. This picture is not static, it varies from moment to moment. For example, one may be violently shaken at the first news of a personal disaster, and for a short moment his thinking may be dominated by a stage I type of reaction, but he may regain his balance very quickly, particularly if he has trained himself in the practice of higher stages. (J. Samuel Bois, *Breeds of Men,* pp. 42-44).

The epistemological profile may be used to great advantage to evaluate a continuous semantic functioning, and, it should be used to take an overall average picture of a person's habitual reaction pattern, and of its changes as he grows by means of modern General Semantics epistemological training or otherwise. Bois wrote in *Explorations in Awareness* (p. 121):

> For a man who lives at stage 2, a project to level 3 or 4 will sound like a useless theory, wild and dangerous. To the man who expects a cure-all from the operational techniques of stage 3, it seems a waste of time and money to invest in the individual development of his key men as required in stage 4. We have noticed that there is in most cases a close relationship between a man's general cultural development and his tendency to function at one stage rather than another.

It is the general level of cultural development of any individual — as it corresponds to definite periods of Western history with the many implications and applications it suggests for self-understanding, self-management, survival and living — that we are concerned about in the epistemological profile. The stages are as follows:

1. *Sensing Stage*

At stage one, Western man took his sensations and feelings as an accurate revelation of what the world was like. His semantic reactions were *evaluative* reactions, and he did not question their objective value. *The world was what* he felt it was, threatening or inviting, beautiful or ugly, depressing or exhilarating, yielding to man's whim or resisting his efforts. Things and events were personified, and ruled by arbitrary gods and spirits whose designs man had to assuage by offerings and sacrifices.

In our twentieth century, people who still react at this sensing stage may not indulge in the religious rites and the magic practices of aborigines but they have retained superstitious practices. They literally believe the astrological column in the daily newspaper; and, they believe the word is the thing, books are gospel and you are either right or wrong.

2. *The Classifying Stage*

The difference between stage one and stage two is not a matter of instruments, it is a matter of what we call "objectivity." It was a great advance when our forefathers took the jump from stage one to stage two. They made the great discovery that the world of nature does not change with the moods of the gods or with man's own reactions. The world of nature has a stability of its own. A thing is identical with itself. It is man's privilege and duty to use his powers of observation and to find the "real" nature of things.

It does not take much observation to see that common-sense theories belong to this stage of cultural development. For men functioning at stage one, things are what they feel they are; for men functioning at stage two, things are what our language *says* they are. Stage-two man is under the impression that the collective brain of his culture mirrors the world: for each word in the dictionary there is a corresponding fact, a thing, a person, an action, or a quality that is somewhere, somehow in the objective world. If his thinking goes from one thought to another according to the rules of logic, he is sure that it goes from one fact to another in the real world. Within his brain there is a miniature of the world, and he is right. There are simple answers to complex questions; and he is right. There are simple answers to complex questions; and people are atheists, communists, Democrats, Republicans, liberals, conservatives, or radicals. People are classified.

3. *The Relating Stage*

When Western man took the semantic jump from stage two to stage three he did not give up his quest for objectivity; in fact, he redoubled the intensity of his drive for a more adequate knowledge of the universe. From the dichotomous language of subject and predicate, of substances and qualities, of agents and actions, he passed to the language of mathematical formulas. The object of his science was no longer *what things are*. It became *what things do* — or better, how they do it.

It meant a strong reaction against whatever smacked of metaphysics, against mere intellectual understanding that does not lead to practical accomplishment. It meant systematic observation and rigorous experimentation both guided by the laws of induction. It meant theories that could lead to further discoveries. The human mind-in-action became attuned to a dynamic universe and developed methods to force nature to reveal its secrets.

It was the age of a science that questioned the authority of the Scriptures and of the philosophers of the past. It was the age of man's coming of age and gradually assuming control over the forces of nature that he was discovering as he was perfecting his methods and his instruments.

If we compare stage two to stage three, we see that the first was just a rough sketch, an oversimplification of the order of nature, a reduction — to a static picture — of the dynamic processes of the world. Stage three in its turn, is now revealed to be an oversimplification of man's relation to the world and to himself. The concept of the reality out there, "of which man is a detached observer, and which he explores and controls with an ever-increasing wisdom, must yield to much more abstract conceptions." (J. Samuel Bois, *Art of Awareness*).

We identify individuals at this stage by their mechanical models. Something is motivated by someone. This stage is used in the present popular concept of power. Relationships being based mostly on who has the most muscle literally, or symbolically. It is the world of the logical positivists and those who separate theory from practice, art from science and metaphysics from hard, cold reality.

4. *The Postulating Stage*

The great discovery that ushered in stage four is the awareness of our self-reflexiveness. We have at last understood that our mental constructs, linguistic or mathematical, are not images of an "objective" world, they are mirrors of ourselves looking at the world. Objectivity, as we took it to be, has now disappeared. Rational absolutes are crumbling. We are actually in the throes of a rebirth to a new form of human life the like of which history has never seen. Reason and rationality have reached their limits, and we are aware of this; proud dogmatism has to make room for humble uncertainty; predictability becomes possibility with an unmeasurable margin of unknowns.

We move from deduction to abduction. Bring metaphysics and empiricism together, relate theory and practice, move from logic to translogic. Examine critically assumptions and premises and develop a non-elementalistic language for understanding the world.

5. *The Unifying Stage*

A stage-five experience takes us out of the established order; it places us in the center of a world where the accustomed signposts of systematic rationality are missing. At the same time, it fills us with an assurance that this is the most genuine experience a human being can have; it is the fountain-head of the greatest achievements and discoveries in all fields of human endeavor: science, religion, philosophy, technology, ethics, law, the fine arts, economics, and politics.

It is labeled the *unifying* stage because creativity involves a certain degree of cosmic consciousness, of felt participation in the energy process that sustains the existence of the whole universe. It is a sharp contrast to the divisive experience of strict objectivity, which we consider so desirable at the layman's level, and to the scientific detachment that we take as the only proper attitude for the sophisticated research worker. (Bois, pp. 114-121, 171-2.)

Dr. Bois has started referring to this stage as the participating stage. I, personally, see a distinction between unifying and participating. I believe they are different orders. To me, the participating stage is dimensional and gives order to the unifying stage. They are different. The participating stage allows us to move into implementation of the unifying experience without reverting to the other stages. We can extensionalize our experience in a vertical fashion. This is the stage for practicing new skills, developing new and creative concepts that build. This way we do not translate the unifying experience into stage two or three activity.

So, I consider it a stage six action which utilizes the extensional methods of modern General Semantics Epistemology. We do not use plain empirical methods for validating our assumptions; we use the overarching process. By doing this we can somewhat disclaim the idea that the epistemological profile is itself a stage 2 methodology.

The epistemological profile *'is'* vertical labeling — making it different from horizontal labeling or labeling in terms of dead level abstracting. The profile is similar to and ties in with the abstracting process and multiordinality. However, one major difference, and it is a difference which makes a difference a *difference,* is that each label is an event and represents (WIGO) what is going on, and a total inference within itself. Another difference is, the epistemological profile process represents semantic jumps rather than a different order of similar activity as multiordinality does. So, within each label or level we would find different orders of abstraction and inferences. It is not to say, however, that the different levels are not to be found operating in the same situation. It is merely that they do not operate simultaneously and it is not just more of the same at a different order of abstraction, but a jump in terms of perception, attitudes and action. Thus, again making it more than a mere stage two activity.

For example, instead of being marooned at the stage of deciding if trying to create a situation of loving my love or hating my hate in order to make multiordinality a reality — so that I won't move to the level of worrying whether I hate — which would be a third level of worrying about whether or not I hate my hate or love my love (See H. Weinberg, *Levels of Knowing and Existence*), I use the epistemological profile to examine the situation without imposing my judgment of whether I should or shouldn't. I use the epistemological profile to examine automatically what is happening to me from the standpoint of the semantic spectrum. It is overarching i.e., multi-ordinal, and the process of abstracting.

Now that we have discussed the backdrop let us move to the stage of implementation. Realizing that a great deal of the how can emerge out of the defining of the what; it is not complete unless there is a circular process tied in with the how at a level where we habitually test the what we have developed and the how we have arrived at; which can be translated as a move from concept to construct. Let us move then from backdrop extensionalization which defines the what and gives us an automatic "how to" way of testing that how, and, provides us with an automatic corrective system.

II. *Extensionalization — Implementation*

Summarized in a few simple formulations, the basic assumption underlying the habits of evaluation, self-management, survival, and living are common to the most advanced contemporary thinkers. The modern habits of evaluation appear to rest on three fundamental non-Aristotelian premises: 1) a map is not the territory — words are not the things they represent; 2) a map does not represent all of a territory — words cannot say all about anything, and; 3) a map is self-reflexive in the sense that an ideal map would have to include a map of the map, which in turn would have to include a map of the map.

A. *Process of Abstracting*

It is the process of abstracting that makes us conscious of this state of affairs. It is this process that General Semantics is fundamentally concerned with. It is this process that enables us to leave the world of 'not' words and to enter the world of words in a manner that coincides with an assumed process, the structure of knowledge, survival, order and the nervous system.

The principles of General Semantics epistemology are statements of the normal functioning of the process. And, what we call semantic disorders are the confusions and inefficiencies that result when these principles are violated. The process of abstracting is an integrated affair. Its organization can be more clearly seen in the form of levels of abstracting.

As we go from one level to the other, certain principles should be kept in mind. We must be aware of the differences between the symbol and symbolized, word and fact, map and territory, speakable and unspeakable. As we go from one level to another, we must hold as our major premises non-identity and non-allness.

The terms non-identity and non-allness are used as follows. There is identity when we identify things, vertically or horizontally, as being the same. For the most part, when the subject-predicate method is used, it is the *is* of identity. On the vertical level, it is identifying different orders of abstractions with each other. It is the identification in talking and acting as if the word were the event and the inference were the description. For example, in Public Administration, when we describe a set of circumstances as comprising span of control, we must be aware that the words will not be able to completely describe that situation and that any assumption to the contrary is but delusion. What, then, should be said? It is not false to use the term as a label as long as it is realized that the term is only a label and does not cover the situation well, the terms non-additive (Korzybski) and structural more (Bois) have been introduced to supply a more complete description of the process which takes place.

The term non-allness simply means that the word does not represent all the object. It is supplementary to the premise of non-identity.

Holding these two terms as fundamental, we find other

subordinate terms coming into play as the process is carried on. Moving from one level to the other, the following terms come into play: assumptions, descriptions, inferences, extensionalism, multiordinal, self-reflexive, self-corrective, non-elementalism, and time-binding.

Man abstracts, and his abstractions are time-binding. That is, his abstractions are passed on from one generation to another, and from one group of workers to another. In dealing with administration, it is well to remember that the information passed on is abstracted.

At this point, something general should be stated about abstracting. A cardinal aspect of the methods of science is the consciousness of the clearest possible statement of one's assumptions. The process of abstracting, thus, proceeds from any particular level upward, then back again to the non-verbal level, then upward and back again. Therefore, the process of abstracting is potentially continuous; it is personal, abstracted from something by someone.

The devices that are outcomes of this process enable us to structure our language and thinking. The devices are indexing, etc., dates, quotation marks and hyphens. Indexing means that we should use indices of some description to indicate that there are differences in terms, statements, things, and people: span of control — 1,2, etc. The etc. is a natural outcome of non-identity and non-allness.

The inculcation of the process of abstracting coupled with the devices mentioned above are supposed to produce the following results in the nervous system:

(1) Probability — This sums up the wisdom that all things are tentative. Truth is tentative because it is abstracted by human beings who are not infallible. All predictions and reports can be given with only some degree of probability, not with absolute certainty.

(2) Delayed reaction — To be conscious of abstracting is to realize that any word or statement, as well as any object or event, is an abstract of something else. In that sense, it is a symbol representing something other than itself. One's reaction,

therefore is to be correspondingly delayed and variable, not too relaxed to act, but, yet, not too tense to be reflexive and flexible. This is non-signal reaction. To the mouse cheese is cheese, that is why mouse traps are effective; he is not discriminating and thus his reflex is conditioned.

(3) Extensionalization — In an extensional orientation, we are aware of differences, as well as similarities. It is extremely easy to see similarities, but in order to see differences, our extensional orientations must be constantly working, looking at the objects instead of assuming sameness.

(4) Projections or conditional terms — These refer to things not as they are, but in recognition of what they seem to be by the observer: examples, to me, in our time, as I see it, it appears to me, it seems.

(5) Plurals — To speak of causes rather than of one cause.

(6) Man as a semantic reactor and transactor.

In summary, we must not confuse General Semantics with Semantics. The difference can be summed thusly. The whole of the Korzybskian system is an outgrowth of Semantics, but the Korzybskian system goes much further. When its implications are worked out, it will be as far removed from semantics as semantics is from logic, and as logic is from grammar. Grammar deals with word-to-word relations. It teaches how to put words together into a sentence. It is not interested in how sentences are related to each other or how they are related to facts. Logic goes further. To a logician, sentences are assertions, and he is interested in relations between assertions (if this is true, then that is true). But for the logician words need not have any meaning except as defined by other words, and the assertions need not have any relation to the world of fact. The semanticist goes further than the logician. To him words and assertions have meaning only if they are related operationally to referents. The semanticist defines not only validity (as the logician does) but also truth. The General Semanticist goes the furthest. He deals not only with words, assertions, and their referents in nature, but also with their effects on human behavior. For a General Semanticist, communication is not merely words in proper order, properly inflected or assertions in proper relation to each other or assertions in proper relation to referents, but all these together, with the chain of fact to nervous system to language to nervous system to action.

III. *Devices*

A. *Extensional Devices*

The practical question comes up immediately: how to train ourselves to evaluate extensionally in terms of the facts, in terms of the processes, rather than intensionally, in terms of the map-definitions alone. These intensional definitions are always fiction. 'Men' and 'women' are fiction. *You* and *you* are not. Our problem is to get out of a 'universe of discourse' where we are dealing with symbols only, into the world of process, where we are dealing with individuals. And, we need to notice both the similarities and the differences.

Korzybski discusses the devices in the introduction to the second edition of *Science and Sanity,* page 28. These devices are methods of self-training in extensionalization: that is, in how to generalize and not to believe your generalizations. You must make them part of you. Here are Korzybski's five specific extensional devices. They are just devices; there is no magic in them; they are just ways of making a human organism orient itself by facts.

EXTENSIONAL DEVICES

Working Devices
1. Indexes. Semanticist_1, Semanticist_2, Semanticist_3, . . ., etc.
2. Dates. X_{1940}, X_{1941}, X_{1942}, . . ., etc.
3. Etc.

Safety Devices
4. Quotes
5. Hyphens

Indexing is a device to ensure that I will talk, not about 'mankind' only, but also about $individual_1$, $individual_2$, $individual_3$, $individual_4$, and so on. Instead of dealing with class names alone and similarities alone, I index each of my terms so that it applies to a definite individual. I then have a flexibility in my terminology: and I have actually an infinite number of words to deal with the infinite number of characteristics which the world presents. I am not confined to a relatively few class names ('man' and 'cat' and 'dog' and 'star', etc.) with which to represent the multitude of unique, individual, changing objects in the world. I now have many, as many as I need. Terms become flexible and definite.

What about the device of dating terms? I know that the world is in constant process. I know that what I am today is not what I was 25 years ago. I know that industrial management today is not what it was 10 years ago. I know that medical practice is not what it was 50 years ago. I know that I, today, am not what I was yesterday or even this afternoon. Each of us is in constant process; everything we observe in the world is dynamic, ever changing. There is no rest. Yet, we have a series of common nouns which assert permanence, emphasize the similarity of the 'same' object yesterday and today.

How can we get out of this linguistic difficulty? We can quit making generalizations without taking in the time factor. Generalizations that we make about 'industry', for example, are often generalizations which we learned from experience in 1920, which we continue to apply today in our thinking, in our evaluation. Suppose that I had an unfortunate experience with you three years ago. Do I know what has happened to you since, or, for that matter, what has happened to me since? I meet you in a new situation. I hated your guts three years ago; how do I behave towards you now? Do I try to find out what has happened to you? Not very often! I still hate your guts. I just don't know anything about you, but I behave as if you were today just as you were before. We can avoid this behavior by using terms *at a date*. You_{1944} are not you_{1941}.

We must make this flexibility in the use of terms, through

indexes and dates, a habitual pattern. These devices focus us on what is going on, (WIGO) on the process-character of nature, where there are *only* absolute individuals in process of change.

Take now the third device: the *permanent* ETC. Remember that we started out here with our mathematical definition of classes, X_1, X_2, X_3, *ET CETERA*. What we have enumerated is *not all*. We need to have it permanently. There are always the factors that we leave out, that we don't have, that we haven't taken account of. What we say will apply to some other things. This device calls our attention to the point that we may have left out; furthermore, it calls our attention to the fact that, whatever we say, we haven't said *everything*. I leave it flexible when I just say *'etc.'* A very different implication, indeed.

We have to remember that, when we make a statement and draw some conclusions from it, we have not drawn from it, even if ours are correct. There are a lot of other things (*etc.*) which we left out.

Korzybski calls these three devices 'working devices.' They are taken directly from mathematics, to achieve in language the flexibility which mathematics achieves by having an infinite number of symbols: $Semanticist_1$, $Semanticist_2$, etc. Such a series of symbols is infinite (this means that I can make it as long as I want): an infinite number of symbols to deal with an infinite variety of characteristics. Then I can date each symbol (X_{1940}) to indicate the process changes in nature. Finally, I can add ETC. to what I say to indicate that I haven't listed everything: there is a lot more.

Korzybski also teaches two other devices, which he calls 'safety devices,' to correct some of the structurally false implications of our language. Notice that we have a lot of words of the sort that we have been investigating: 'mind' and 'body' and 'space' and 'time' — a kind of word which is very useful. You can use these words as powerful investigating tools: but only if you know, very thoroughly and completely, that what they indicate is fiction; only if you don't believe a word that is said.

How can we get away from the notion that these elementalistic terms represent realities in the universe? Put them in quotation marks. Not necessarily always on the paper, although it is probably better to do so since the quotes bring out the fictional character of the term to your reader. Put the quotes on the term in your own head, anyway. If you use elementalistic terms, *never* draw a conclusion from them, because that conclusion will contain the structure of the metaphysics which surround the term. Use them when you have to: but draw your conclusions from the process fact, if your conclusions are going to "be worth" anything.

Lastly, the device of hyphens. Our language is so shot through with different elementalistic words, which reflect elementalistic unconscious assumptions, that we have to do something very definite to bring things together which are together in life, but which are a long way apart in the traditional ways of knowing which the language mirrors. For example, take the problem we are studying, the problem of general semantics. Now, in a college catalogue, the department of English deals with semantics; the department of Anatomy deals with neurology on one level; the department of Psychology deals with neurology on another level; the department of Psychiatry deals with it on another level. They are all 'separate subjects'; yet the reactions which they study are not separate in us.

One way to bring these matters closer to ourselves, one way to show ourselves that these 'separate' things are really together, is to use terms like 'neuro-semantic', where you bring traditionally discrete things together, to the unity that they are in reality. 'Space-time', 'psychosomatic medicine', are such terms. The things referred to are together in reality, why not put them together in the term?

These devices are designed to make more flexible our use of the pictures which we have in our maps and our high-order generalization. They will help us avoid elementalism and silent linguistic assumptions, so that we can use new premises; help us achieve extensionalization, the ability to deal with the facts of the situation and not exclusively with whatever we are pleased to say about the situation.

I can do anything with the maps whatsoever. But the territory is not affected in the least. I can write volumes about the 'human mind' in the abstract. It isn't going to affect the way you behave in the least. Because I may say that you are Body plus Mind, it does not follow that you are split into the elementalistic concepts which I have spoken about. Any conclusion that I draw on the basis of this 'concept' of mine is just a conclusion within my made-up logical universe. It does not control the processes that unfold.

We must at the same time make our map self-reflexive. It gives the map-territory analogy a semantic twist that changes the whole picture. Humankind does not simply perceive as a camera perceives what it is focused upon; he perceives *self-reflexively.* As a semantic transactor, time-bound in a cultural heritage expressed mostly in the language he has learned to speak, he has first-order experiences mostly in the language he has learned to speak, he has first-order experiences that emerge in a definite pattern. This pattern has the multi-dimensional structure of his semantic state at the moment. It involves attitudes, feelings, purposes, habits, electro-chemical conditions, anticipations of the future and pressures from the last. It is not merely a process of making a more or less accurate map of an assumed territory, the features of which would determine the characteristics of the map he is tracing. It is a matter of knowing that we are involved which makes the map subjective not objective.

IV. *The Transaction in Process: A Transition*

By using this formulation we do not reduce the complex to the simple. We substitute a complexity more intelligible. Substitute the involved but comprehensible for the uninvolved and incomprehensible. Seek complexity and order it.

The concept of culture has its input on the concept of man. When seen as a set of symbolic devices for controlling behavior, extra-somatic sources of information, culture provides the link between what men are intrinsically capable of becoming and what they actually, one by one, in fact become. Becoming human, becoming individual under the guidance of cultural patterns. Historically created a system of meaning in terms of which we give form, order and direction to our lives.

A. *Application*

The humanizing of the administrative and physical science process in recent years has brought greater attention to what man ought, can, and might do. Perhaps, the greatest problem is how to change the actual behavior pattern of individual and groups.

Training people are, almost universally, searching for sound and economical ways to find what ought to be taught and how to teach it.

The methodology does not include memorizing the rules of General Semantics rotely. Each rule is designed to point beyond itself to the sub-level. They were intended as a discipline of the senses, emotions and the mind — the organism as a whole. Continued application of the rules would gradually liberate the individual from his previous orientation. The fears and misconceptions that each might have about the wishes and motives of others, creating conditions favorable to solving realistic and mutual problems.

The subject-predicate form, the *is* of identity, and the elementalism of the Aristotelian system, not understanding man as a semantic transaction, failure to understand man's epistemological development and an overarching framework not in keeping with effective time-binding, are perhaps the main semantic factors in need of revision and elaboration as they are found to be the foundation of the insufficiency of this system and represent the mechanism of semantic disturbance, making general adjustments and sanity impossible.

Instead of the *is* of identity, we use the best available language, namely, an actional, behavioristic, functional, operational language that is based on order. The term used is an abstraction of different orders. It is functionally satisfactory and has a non-elementalistic way of approaching the necessary communicative areas.

It is always advisable to introduce terms which are structurally close to our daily experiences. It must be granted, however, that the introduction of any new language is generally perplexing and is justified only if the new language accomplishes something structurally and semantically which the old did not accomplish. In this case, it has brought us to a new and sharp distinction between man and animal. This difference may be called the *horizontal* difference. The solution of the majority of human semantic difficulties and the elimination of pathological identification lie in the ability to differentiate between horizontal levels of abstractions. The animal does not know that he abstracts and cannot know because he differentiates only in a vertical level.

If man organizes a complex organization and his semantic reactions are adjusted only to the simpler animal kind of structures, then communication becomes difficult. All human experience, 1971, shows that he still copies animals in his nervous reaction of trying to adjust himself to a world of fictitious, simple animal structure, while actually, he lives in a different world which is humanly complex.

The vertical stratification not only gives representation for the sharp difference between man and animal, but it also allows the training of semantic reactions in individuals. The present theory can only be fully beneficial when one acquires in his system the habitual feeling of both the vertical and horizontal stratification with which identification becomes possible. This can be done in two ways: (1) by showing the abstracting from the event to the object, and then applying a name to the object; (2) by illustrating the level of statements which can be made about statements.

The structural differential shows that the objective level of life is not words, and cannot be reached by words alone. The semantic reactor of Bois is a revision of the structural differential. We need to study and master both conceptually and from the standpoint of personal constructs.

The whole of the present theory can be illustrated on the

structural differential by the childishly simple operations of the trainer pointing a finger to the event and then to the object saying this is not this and insisting on silence on the part of the trainees. One should continue by showing, with the finger, the object and the label, saying again "This is not this," insisting on the objective level; then, showing the first and the second label, saying again this is not this.

It can also be done with the semantic reactor-transactor by internalizing its meaning and through the overarching process by philosophical commitment.

B. *What It Takes*

It takes time to use, habitually and spontaneously, this complete picture of man as the foundation of our practical knowledge of ourselves and our fellow human beings. Our language does not help this new orientation; it is elementalistic. It assumes that thoughts, feelings, bodily movements, and biochemical exchanges within our tissues and endocrine glands are relatively independent phenomena. In modern General Semantics epistemology they are neither independent nor dependent in a cause-and-effect relation, they are aspects of one complex process which becomes our real unit of observation and discourse. Instead of saying "I think", "I feel", "I move", which are elementalistic terms — we have to say to ourselves "I react semantically." This means that my whole organism, reacts at all levels to assert the values I hold dear. In practice, we often use the word react, asking people who share the description of man "How do you *react* to this or that?" Instead of "What do you *think* of this?" or "How do you *feel* about that?"

The difference may appear slight at first, mere quibbling; but if one takes time to ponder over it he will recognize that it is one of those differences that makes a great deal of difference.

Finally, the world in which we live may be seen as a world of semantic reactions and transactions.

V. *The Process in Action: Some Examples*

A. *The Epistemological Profile in Action*

The following is an example which illustrates the use of the epistemological profile and also the development of a philosophical commitment emerging out of the overarching process.

It was a while before I became aware of a certain process which was taking place. In reflection I think about Malcolm X. There was in my life, a parallel. Malcolm went through many changes. He moved from ethnocentric to transactive relationships. Tracing this on the epistemological profile he moved from the sensing, classifying to the relating stage — after undergoing a peak experience which was level five. His peak experience was translated into stage three, the relating stage. He was on the move when he died.

I had a similar experience after being deeply involved in the cause of Blacks and a search for Black identity, relating very closely to the community through the Black Congress. I became deeply ethnocentric and 'hated' white people. After the Panthers were killed at UCLA many of us were slated or marked for death, because many of us had been involved in the efforts of the Black Congress. The members began to blame each other for what had happened. (I am now indulging in the science of the process — a higher level of abstraction beyond the process itself — multiordinality.) At that point, unconsciously, as Malcolm X did, I began to re-evaluate my life, where I was going, and what I wanted to die for. Following this I had a peak experience in New York, as outlined in Position Paper #5. At that point I lifted my sights and became less ethnocentric and more committed to Black identity as a working model for developing broader concepts for deprived and oppressed people of all colors and at all levels. I found a new significance and meaning. My sights were lifted and fears diminished. I knew what I would die for; because, then I knew what I would live for, i.e., elimination of oppression in a universal sense. I realized that our future — the Black that is, was tied in with that of all who wanted to create and give new direction to a world in trauma. I believe, in reflection that Malcolm X had a similar experience — when he was "kicked" out of the Muslim temple. He too, moved to new levels. By using the Epistemological Profile we are able to trace these developments. One other discovery is made when the profile is used — the non-rational, sub-microscopic non-verbal process which moves one to a peak experience and semantic jump, it seems that only in reflection do we understand the process that leads to the peak experience. It is most important that we accept the changes and wait for knowledge to come which will reveal the 'natural' process. In some cases we must call this a motive, a stimulus, or some other verbal process. This is an oversimplification. It is a process which reveals itself in partial form — in linear form if you will — but only partially so, after the experience. My major point here is that experience moves us to new levels and we can only understand it in part at a later date. The important thing is that we allow the experiences to emerge. This is the way we develop our philosophical commitment. Out of this emerges the how of an operation. Another example has to do with social action in general. This not only illustrates a set of values, but the emergence of a direction evolving out of the process.

B. *General Semantics Epistemology as a Social Action Change Process*

How do we handle the present social unrest and social action in the future? Usually the answers are: give the people a chance to participate in the democratic process; give the disaffected a chance to channel their energies along lines that will make for peaceful change; give the alienated a part to play; let us integrate the races and let us allow each group to do its thing; let us examine psychologically the dissatisfied in terms of low level psychological classifications, i.e., they are angry at their parents; they are taking their personal frustrations out on society. These are assumptions and inferences, part of a process, at the present time we cannot begin to know. Then what do we offer? We should go back to Alfred Korzybski, and begin to push wherever we are, a new process — begin wherever we are developing this process in terms of Neil Postman's and Weingartner's assumptions of the creative process and their method of inquiry

(*Teaching as a Subversive Activity.*)

Start with the outline in Manhood of Humanity and move to the process of Teaching as Subversive Activity. At that point we will begin to give rise to direction; a new direction from where we are no longer a party to the conspiracy, but are epistemological functionaries.

It should be done by individuals of that breed. We must start someplace. I lack the desire at this point to start with the terms that we must make the nation change their practices with words. We must start with the assumption personally, that we will not be a party to the conspiracy. How do we do this? The illustration given by Ed Connerly, a doctoral student in one of our special Seminars was "I see program value in the General Semantics process by using the first generation tools and techniques." His ideas are to get those out to people on a pragmatic basis. I had not given consideration to this before then, now I do. Let me say what ingredients I think the process should contain:

1. The medium is the message.
2. The first semantic tools and techniques where and "how", they should be utilized.
3. Second generation tools and techniques "where" and "how" they should be utilized.
4. Then,
    a. My major concern is how do we build a systemic framework which automatically enables us to move forward as in quantum mechanics?
    b. How do we come to a philosophical commitment that things are temporary?

This should be the framework which would produce action. This in no way says we should not utilize the tools and techniques of General Semantics no matter what generation — but, it means that we combine the tools and project ourselves into the arena of knowing. We must be systematic. I find that the best way to systematize is through modern epistemology. In each situation, we must sit down and try to think of new and creative concepts in view of differences and similarities relative to other situations that appear to be similar, e.g., take the postal union strike. They should have started with the idea that they could not negotiate based on the old private enterprise economic model, but engaged creatively in a process to determine how they should negotiate. I believe an engagement based on an old economic model kept the historical process and trend from making the geometric changes necessary and bringing our social affairs in line with our technology. We did not allow the epistemic process to develop, naturally. In order to do that we must begin methodologically with the assumption that "this is a new situation, a chance for creative action". Our starting question then would be what methods and processes should we use? Instead of what kind of agreements should we reach in terms of the old methods. The method of inquiry of the process becomes important and keeps us in line with geometric, quantum, and the epistemic processes. (So called 'natural' processes — sub-microscopic — See Bridgeman, *The Way Things Are* and Bois, *Breeds of Men.*)

VI. *Preliminary Word*

But knowing about man is not enough. Socrates' prescription, "Know thyself," will be put in the museum of antiquities with the logic of Aristotle and the ideas of Plato unless it is translated into rules on conduct. In this, as in any other field of endeavor, the time has come to pass from *knowing-what-it-is* to *knowing-what-to-do-with-it,* from science to technology, from theory to practice. (J. Samuel Bois, *The Art of Awareness,* p. 264.)

Realizing the potential and promise of man and providing leadership and direction which emphasize a reverence for man and commit us to living rather than surviving, provides hope and confidence for the future.

It must be remembered that we have been taught a non-process system, which involves the "is" of identity, and a static view of the world. So we do confuse orders of abstraction.

Preparing for ourselves and the children, predispositions for bursting into speech instead of waiting a moment or delaying action.

Training in the General Semantics epistemological process gives a maximum probability that the organism-as-a-whole will be affected. In this way, an intellectual theory engages the senses and feelings and reflex mechanisms. To affect the organism-as-a-whole, organism-as-a-whole methods must be used.

People dislike training repeatedly, but it is impossible to acquire structural familiarity with typing or driving a car by verbal means alone. Without the active training with the differential, the best results cannot be expected. Only the semantic training with differential in non-identity can affect the habitual and the unconscious.

The principles involved here are often childishly simple, often generally known to the point that some people feel offended when we fuss over them. But we must remember that no matter how much these simple principles are approved of verbally, in no case are they fully applied in practice, because all of us are trained in a linguistic and semantic system based on identity. This infantile identification will unconsciously play havoc with all our semantic reactions unless this blockage is counteracted.

Summary

Again, from one point of view, the General Semantics epistemological process methods are childishly simple. Most of us say, "I already know this." We do. Most of us practice some of it, but none of us use all of it, and very few are aware of the complete process that takes place. Consequently, our awareness is shoddy and erratic because of the power of old, established habits. If it were systematic and made us conspicuously conscious of the entire abstracting process and its implications, we would be moving toward a saner approach to organizational and world problems. The problem then is to become aware of a process which teaches us that we may analyze problems in a scientific, intellectual way, involving our feelings and intuitions. This approach leads to a psychophysiological approach based on order. Thus the structurally necessary translations of one level of abstractions into the other and vice versa, is enormously facilitated. What is the overall effect of this? The most workable feature consists in the fact that being based on such fundamental principles as *non-identification, non-elementalism,* and an overarching process, it has an organic unity.

The General Semantics epistemological process is a source of understanding the world about us. It applies to all phases of life and disciplines, e.g., psychiatry, mathematics, physics, psychology, business, teaching, law, and social sciences, etc. It is the task of interested people in perspective disciplines to bring this material to the attention of their colleagues. It is not uniquely appropriate to one discipline, but rather it is uniquely appropriate to all in that it is language, and it is a dimension of epistemology with a process orientation, and it pervades life and enables men to work at their professions. Therefore, it has a place in Public Administration, and as we see it, application will be helpful.

This is a beginning not an end.

VII. *General Semantics Epistemological Framework — Summary Case*

1. General Semantics Process — Introduction

   A. Language dimension of epistemology

   B. Man as a time-binder — What does this mean?

   C. First Generation — See Korzybski

      1. Process of abstracting — first generation tools and techniques
      2. Non-identity
      3. Non-allness
      4. Non-elementalism
      5. The indexes — hyphens
      6. Differences that make a difference

7. Multi-ordinality
8. Extensionalization
9. Non-additive
10. Map vs. territory

D. Second Generation Tools — Bois

1. The Epistemological Profile — See Bois, *Art of Awareness, Breeds of Men*

E. Third Generation

1. Williams

a. Overarching frame of reference
b. Science of the process
c. Theory of the process
d. The process — Language dimension
e. Vehicles
f. Hoisting
g. Personal constructs
h. Extensionalization — Backdrop
i. A difference which makes a difference a *difference*
j. One man theory

2. Bois

a. Transaction in process
b. Central assembly
c. Map — territory (Dynamic and self-reflexive)
d. Epistemic process

3. Liebig, Mark

a. Special empirical testing

4. Kenneth Johnson, Morris, Postman, Weingartner, and others.

a. Philosophical direction
b. Philosophy

CHAPTER XV

NEW DIMENSIONS IN MEANING: RENEWAL OF SELF AND COMMUNITY

This is a transcript of a speech delivered at a Conference on *New Dimensions in Meaning, Renewal of Self and Community* at Benedict College, Columbia, South Carolina. Benedict is an all Black liberal arts institution. The speech was delivered from a few notes making it largely extemporaneous. Only minor grammatical corrections were made in this copy, so as to keep the informal nature of this speech.

William J. Williams
Los Angeles, California

Tonight I would like to share with you some feelings I have about some things. At the center of those things might be Black Economic Development. We can use that as a starting point. I suppose I could classify what I am going to say as an attitude; I would like to share an attitude with you. I would like to share some feelings with you about some things that relate to our general theme, our general subject, and my own particular topic. Consequently, I take my cue from the theme "New Dimensions in Meaning and Renewal of Self and Community," that topic struck me as being very timely. When I read it, I thought about Kenneth Boulding and his "New Dimension" and I thought about John Gardner and his "Self Renewal" and other similar writings. All of these ideas tend to come to mind when we begin to see works like that. They are very popular at the moment. Just as the word *relevant* is. We have our own ways of looking at these popular terms, but they do hold some general meaning. However, they do need some clarifying, so I am going to concentrate mostly on the *new dimensions and self-renewal of self and the community.*

From this theme will emerge my attitude concerning Black Economic Development. I think you'll understand this as I look at economic development. It seems to me that when we begin to use words like *new dimensions,* and *self-renewal,* we are talking about some new directions, we are talking about some correct methodology. What kind of methodology are we talking about? We, in the School of Public Administration at the University of Southern California have had sort of a discussion about the fields of phenomenology, general semantics, and epistemology. And as we discussed these subjects and began to look into them, I found out that one of the basic things that separate the various philosophies or the "ologies", as we call them, was the methodology. Correct methodology that can stand the test of time, is what we are looking for. On the surface, they all seem very similar. Phenomenology reaches a high level like Zen Buddhism or like the existentialists. But all of these have something in common. Even in the fields of Sociology and Anthropology, we try to reach a new level. But the one thing we seem to fall short on is how to get there, how to reach that new level.

I want to talk a little about that tonight. I don't have the time or the familiarity with all that I would like to say in order to develop it as fully as I would like to. But I would like to share something with you, some thoughts that I have on that particular subject, i.e., how to reach new levels. Let me start with Harold Cruse and his *Crisis of the Negro Intellectual.* Harold Cruse said in that book that we cannot have Black economic development until the Blacks control economics of their particular community; until profits that are earned in that community are plowed back into that community; that Black economic development, as far as a Black community is concerned, means looking at some new economic forms. He talks about enterprises that are collectively owned, cooperatives that are collectively owned, as well as state-sponsored economic organizations. Then he goes on to make another statement in that same book (if you haven't read it, perhaps you ought to). He said that the dilemma that we face is based on the Constitution. In the Constitution, it is said that the individual is supreme, but in our political institutions we have a tendency to emphasize the "group"; therefore, he concludes, we need Black solidarity.

All the races and all the religions have some kind of group structure, and this country speaks to groupism; not the individual but groupism. And here is the gap between theory and practice in many areas. So, he proposes the hypothesis that we must have a deep kind of commitment in our community. Black people must solidify their efforts and come together, and forget the ideal of individualism because it doesn't work. Consequently, those who have subscribed to that, he said, have serious trouble in functioning in this society. He says this is a figment of the American imagination: that the individual is supreme. There is another need.

Now what does Black Economic Development mean to me? Let me share something of what I think it means and the way I feel. In 1967, if I had spoken to you, I would have marooned myself at the individual level. I would have committed myself to that theory, that philosophy, and said that's where it is and that's what we have got to do. In 1967, you couldn't talk to me about anything but Black; Black identity, Black involvement, Black commitment. I couldn't see anything else. But as we go through this therapeutic experience, many things happen. We begin to relate to ourselves, we begin to develop and wear the naturals, stop using bleaching creams and all that sort of thing; but, something happened. I completed my teaching semester at the University, and I went to New York to serve as a consultant to the New York Port Authority. I could feel some things happening to me during that summer that had not happened to me before. I did not know what it was; I felt very upset. I felt low and kind of depressed. You see we even describe our experiences in low psychological terms. We become marooned at that level and then we run to a psychiatrist because we think that's where our problems are; and sometimes it's because we don't have a significance or a meaning in life — that becomes the main thing sometimes; but we can talk about that later. But I had an experience in New York City, and I will make this as brief as I can.

We were going to put on a Black Development Conference at the University of Southern California and I got a letter from the American Assembly and from the Director of the School of Public Administration. The Director wanted me to be a Co-director of the conference. Something about that at that time bothered me. I had been talking Black all year. All of my experiences were along that line. I couldn't see anything else. Why, all of a sudden did I get this feeling that I had to think about this? Wasn't this after all what I wanted all along? When he sent me the letter about sponsoring a Black Economic Development Conference at the University of Southern California under the auspices of the American Assembly, I had to think about it overnight. See, ideas don't come to us all at once and that may be the difference between creative thinking and rote memory. In rote memory, we begin to analyze all kinds of problems and throw them out there and say, "what alternative should I choose?" instead of relating to ourselves and perhaps letting something come out and emerge, this becomes the creative part. That's another thing I'm going to talk about later on.

Then about two days later I was walking down 14th Street in New York, about noontime, and as I rounded the block I got a flash. Now those of you who are ministers might know what I mean. I guess other people have had revelations. But all of a sudden I felt as if I were having an experience that I had never had before. It was a bright, sunny day in New York City in spite of all the debris and the pollution and the degradation, or whatever you want to call it. But in that city, all of a sudden I saw a bright light and I FELT SOMETHING that I had never felt before. I felt that I saw the word *system.* I visualized the word system. And, then I visualized a couple of other words — "the system had to go". You see, I had been relating to the whole thing as if it were an institution. All of a sudden, now I thought about system. I had used the words institution and systematizing before but they had never hit me in my gut like it did that day. I felt deeply committed at that point, to the idea that the system had to go. And, those of you who have had, and we all have experiences I think, have learned this just as I have related it to you. We all do it, it's whether or not we are aware and we allow these revelations to take place within us, and then relate to them. I knew the kind of answer I would have to that letter. So I felt ten feet tall. For example, my friends, my family, and even death took a certain new kind of relationship in my life. My fears seemed to pass away from me. I was beginning to feel committed to something at long last. As long as I was thinking just Black I didn't get this feeling; I had a feeling but it wasn't spiritual, if you will it was ethnocentric and narrow. I got a spiritual feeling that it was larger than just the Black thing that we were so concerned about. We were concerned about the system and the institutions that comprise that system. So, for days, I felt very high, very good as though I were on top of everything and things seemed to fall in place. And you know, I had heard many people say, you've got to have something to live for and if you do, you're not afraid of dying. At that point I thought about death, and I didn't feel the kind of fear I had felt before. So I had had an experience and I felt committed.

I then answered the letter and said to the Director that I would participate, if you're not just talking about *Black* business and training *Black* managers. Because if you're talking about putting together Black capitalistic enterprises in a Black community to dehumanize Black people, then I don't want any part of it. If we are going to just transplant White economic concepts that have dehumanized White people, into the Black community, I want no part of it. Because to me it seems we ought to be able, at this point in our lives, to transcend that if we're talking about new dimensions and new meaning. So this took me smack into the arena of social action. I wrote him and we had a long dialogue about that, (I'm going to conclude this in a moment). I insisted that you can keep your questions in there regarding the training of Black managers and all the other Black concerns; maybe that's one level, but there are several other levels and it seems to me we have a bigger responsibility, one of developing concepts for the whole nation or for the total society. If we don't accept that responsibility, then we are not doing our jobs. So we included some questions concerning the legitimacy of our own system. That was one of the questions, and we added about four other questions. I have sought to indicate that when we begin to talk about new dimensions, when we begin to talk about self-renewal of community, that we are not just talking about the Black community, we are talking about the whole society because it seems to me that our society is in deep trouble.

How then do we begin? (Now I'm sharing with you some of my experiences and the values I hold dear, and that's all a teacher can do). You see when you are in a classroom, you can't really teach people, but you can engage in a process. And those of us who think we are teaching something have missed the boat. That's rote memory. We are not being effective *Time Binders*. If we are true time binders, then we are engaged in a process where we all begin to learn together. The teacher becomes a student. We should assume that kind of humility in the classroom, that's frequently what the students are talking about when they talk about relevance. They are talking about engaging in a process where we all begin to learn together in 1971 and project forward. So we talk about new dimensions and new meanings.

If we are going to talk about that, then we are going to have to talk about the concept of change. And if we're going to talk about the concept of change, we have to put that within some kind of frame of reference. I taught courses in change, The Administrator in Social Conflict, The Administrative Process and Social Change, etc., not even knowing what I was talking about for a very long time, because I had no feel for it. — I did though have a concept of change. A concept being different from having a feel. Now change could mean anything. It could mean moving from one side of the room to the other, it could mean moving from deductive-inductive reasoning to inductive-deductive reasoning and you're still within the same kind of logical system. You haven't moved anywhere, that's just a change without a difference. But we want to talk about a difference that makes a difference.

One night I was struggling with this concept and I was doing it in a mechanical fashion. I began to lay it out — what are the alternatives? — see that's rote memory stuff, that's the way I was taught in school. They taught in school. They taught me not to relate to myself, all of my papers were well documented with footnotes and that sort of thing. It didn't speak to *me,* and this is very important, when it begins to speak to you, you forget about the documentations and say where you are coming from, what is your value system, where you stand on the subject, not what someone else has said. So I began to relate in that fashion to the concept of change.

Then one night, I had a dream (not a nightmare — it was really a dream). And I woke up the next morning and went into the bathroom and started shaving. I then recalled vividly, the dream, I dreamed that I was in a classroom, and I was a student in the classroom, not a teacher, I always try not to assume a teacher role anyway. So I was looking towards the front of the room with everyone else and there was somebody who had his back to us while we were all talking about change in a mechanical fashion; we were discussing it very intelligently, very intellectually, intellectualizing the total process. And then he turned around all of a sudden and said "Bull, this is not what you're talking about. You're not talking about change you are talking about growth." Now the word change began to make sense when I felt it in terms of growth. I had been passing on bad information to my classes about change, without really coming to grips with what I was talking about because the question, "change from what to what?" becames very important when you talk about change. Change is a high level abstraction and it doesn't specify where we are. But when you begin to talk about growth, change began to make real sense to me. And at that point I did something else — you see, I do a lot of things on my own because they make sense to me — then I began to make a distinction between a construct and a concept.

A concept is something out there. It is a mechanical operation, when I begin to relate to something that makes some sense, that I can feel in the pit of my stomach, something that emerges out of the situation, then I consider that a construct. And I began to develop a personal construct about what we meant by change. The concept of growth began to make some sense to me in general, and when I equated it with the concept of change, it began to make even more sense.

We cannot deal with economic development, any kind of economic development without considering the concept of power. The rhetoric of Black power has to be implemented. One of the students at USC came in to me one day when a Black leader was making a big speech on campus, and said "You know, I heard Uncle Tough Talk out there today." He didn't say Uncle Tom he said "Uncle Tough Talk. . . ." Then he referred to him as the man in the gray-flannel dashiki. So we use a lot of rhetoric. The real question though is whether or not we are going to move into action and begin to do something. That's what he was talking about. He said, "It's time we started doing and stopped using the rhetoric." We need to take a new look at the concept of power. What does *power* mean?

One day as I was walking across the campus, something came to me and I started thinking about vehicles. I am the Director of the Center for Social Action and I was very depressed about what we were doing. We were supposed to train so many people in the community to be effective, to do organizing and all that sort of thing. And, in spite of the fact that we were satisfying the foundations and the government, I wasn't very pleased with what we were doing. I had a very narrow idea about goals. I was trying to follow the book in terms of implementation. Then, as I was walking across the campus, the concept, now the construct, of vehicles came to me. And I started applying that to what I was doing. We have, and I've just made a discovery, we have more power right where we are than we realize when we begin to conceive of things as vehicles; when we begin to move from one level to another; when we have an overarching kind of framework, a place where we want to go and at the lower level certain things become vehicles. So, at that point the Center for Social Action became a place where I would house the Black Student Union, the Chicano group, the Asian American Alliance, and the Kennedy Action Corps. All of the groups that had some relevance. And even, welcomed, the YAF, the Young Americans for Freedom, if they wanted to work, and they do sometimes, on some things. So they were all housed there, and I began to see the Center for Social Action as a vehicle for bringing about this growth I was talking about. I no longer looked at it in a very narrow sense. And then I felt somewhat powerful. Then I extended that and I began to look at the School of Public Administration and the University of Southern California and all of those things as a vehicle for getting somewhere. Where? To the point of trying to relate to an overarching kind of social action which would bring about change, then these vehicles become incidental to the total process. Benedict College is a vehicle for bringing about change. If you begin to look at it as an end in itself, you miss the point. Then you forget what kind of power you have in your grasp for bringing about change.

We must, it seems to me, in addition to that, begin to use symbolism. I deal in a lot of symbolism, right or wrong, this is where I am, to a large extent. Now what do I mean by symbolism? Let me give you one example. In the School of Public Administration, we have a Planning Committee. In one meeting we talked about bringing minorities into the School. You don't have that problem, do you? Well, anyway we have that problem, you see. How many minorities are we going to have in the School of Public Administration? How many scholarships are we going to grant to minorities? I had a similar confrontation with the Department before, so consequently, I felt as if it were going to be a useless exercise, this time, to even discuss it. Somebody raised the question, "Well what are you going to do about the poor White people? It's unfair to poor White people?" Back in 1968 we had raised the question at the School of Public Administration regarding the certifying of interns into Southern California municipalities. At that time I raised a question, I said, a fellow from Glendale came by, he was a personnel Director, and he said to me "can you send me a black engineer, I said well, what about a Black accountant or a Black management intern?" He said, "Well I think they'll have a problem adjusting in Glendale" . . . . I said that's certainly not your problem, let him have that problem adjusting. Well, anyway, that stimulated me to think about the internship program we had there. We were certifying interns to municipalities that were engaging in discrimination. They were saying they didn't want a Chicano, they didn't want an Asian, they wanted a White one. So I started addressing myself to this issue. I went before the Policy Committee. The question I raised was, if we are going to certify interns to a municipality we ought to have them sign an affidavit saying that they will not discriminate. Sign it, put it in writing. Some of the professors had a vested interest in many of the municipalities; they did their consultant work for them, they had relationships with them, so they still believed in the process of accommodation. As we fussed and argued, one of the faculty members, there were about 13 of us, I was the 13th, turned to me and he said, we're not against you, you know that. *We* are not against *you*. Then it comes home to you, then you realize how foreign you are. So anyway he's saying we could accomplish it through accommodation. I couldn't understand anybody in 1968 talking about accommodation. Accommodation does not work. It has not worked up to now, perhaps when our mentalities and our mental constructs change, perhaps it will, but it has *not* to the extent that we could begin to adjust ourselves at that level to the process of accommodation. So they said, "You are talking about confrontation." I said yes, that's exactly what I'm talking about, conflict and confrontation. And he said, "If you were a little milder about what you are doing; if you took the position that we could have some kind of compromise, then perhaps we could talk about what you are talking about and get some results." I said no, I think we have to get it a certain way and if we don't get it a certain way, it's not worth having.

Well, it so happens that I prevailed in that particular instance. We sent it out and the municipalities were glad to sign the affidavit. They said fine, and were glad to see the University of Southern California at long last take some positive action. You know, a lot of the things we fear are in our minds. And the *Los Angeles Times* came out and wrote an article of commendation. But anyway, I wanted to get it through a certain way. So when we came to the minority question of how many we were going to get into the School and whether or not we were going to set aside X number of grants for minority students, we had to say minority students because we've got the Chicanos and the Asian-Americans out there. And so, the Chairman came to me and said, "Now I know how you operate, I would like to get this through. We have an excellent opportunity of getting this through the committee. If you will make your presentation without confronting the groups." And I said that it is symbolically necessary for me to confront that group in every case simply because we are not just talking about getting X number of scholarships for X number of minority students, Blacks and so forth. We are talking about a re-education program and you have got to put everybody through a process so they will know exactly the kind of commitment they are making. And if you do it that way, you do it on the basis of a theoretical principle and when you come back again you won't have to travel the same road. So he said "With your symbolism we are not going to get it through." And I said, I'll stay away from the meeting if you're anxious just to get that through because I have to confront as I go along, this is very necessary for me to do because this is the way I look at it and symbolism is very important to me. So I'm saying that I think in order to do a great deal of this we have to use symbolism in order to get things done. We cannot separate, for example, the means from the ends we are trying to accomplish. I think if we do that, we miss the point about the arena of social change.

The one thing that is very hard to do when we begin to talk about this total change process, this new area, and the transcendence of certain kinds of things to get somewhere, is to mention poor people. Now if you really want to get people up tight, you begin to talk about poor people in a very elementary kind of way, where it really counts, where you are going to make some kind of decision. I happened to be on the Executive Committee of the Faculty Senate at USC. And this is the kind of discussion we had. We sat down and talked about tuition remission for poor people, for Black people, for Asians, for poor people. And, then the discussion became an ideological one; they began to talk about Socialism versus Capitalism; and that USC is not a state institution, it is a private institution; therefore, we can't take certain monies and spend them on scholarships, we were doing that anyway, indirectly, but we were spending it in a different area. What they were really saying, is that we don't want all those poor people here. When you begin to talk about more than just Black people, you begin to talk about an entirely new dimension. You begin to attack the basic values of the country because we don't like poor people. This, I am saying, ties in with some of our new social concerns. A fellow by the name of Alfred Korzybski came up with a phrase (or term), that he called time-binding. He said, "You know, we have missed something about man, and it is this, that we have confused him with animals and with plants. We have not made a distinction between man and animals as yet. Until we straighten out that confusion, we are going to be in trouble because most of the things we do are based on the assumption that man is like an animal—most of our metaphors." Korzybski said, "Man is not an animal because an animal is a space binder; man is not a plant because plants are energy-binders; but man is a time-binder." Man symbolizes, conceptualizes, and passes knowledge on from one generation to the other. That makes him a time-binder and not a space-binder. And when we begin to relate to that, you see, we also have to move to another dimension and away from zoology. In the classrooms we are keepers of the animals. In our institutions, in our prisons, wherever we are, our economic institutions are based on zoology and not man as a time-binder. Now, everybody, of course is a time-binder.

What makes one person more effective as a time-binder than another? Two fellows named Postman and Weingartner wrote a book called *Teaching as a Subversive Activity*. They say this: anytime you pass knowledge on historically, the grammar that we used to know — the mathematics that we once knew, the chemistry that we once knew, the physics, the social sciences — anytime you pass that knowledge on without questioning the basic assumptions underlying that knowledge; you are an ineffective time-binder. This is usually what we do in the classrooms. We don't question the underlying assumptions. We take it for granted that what was written is correct. Nouns are very static, they do not speak to change and we usually just use nouns. In the future instead of saying mind, say minding, instead of education, educating then it becomes a process and non-static. Our grammar does not allow us to do this. So the one who questions the validity of old concepts in the classroom and relates them to a process, is an effective time-binder. The ineffective ones are talking about rote memory. The effective ones talk about something that may be related to creativity.

How do we adjust ourselves to these new dimensions; to this self-renewal? It seems to me that we have got to develop an over-arching kind of framework; a process. We have got to begin to look at differences that make a difference. There is a fellow by the name of J. Samuel Bois, who wrote a book called *The Art of Awareness* and in that book he talks about different breeds of men; and, then he wrote another one entitled *Breeds of Men* where he expanded the concept. And in that he said that we have passed through five stages in our development. The sensing stage, which is very primitive; the classifying stage — where people classify you — you're either a Communist or you're not a Communist — you're either a Socialist or you're a Capitalist. We classify without really getting a deep understanding; Then he moves on, to a third level, the relating level — where power relationships become the important kinds of things and considerations; he says there is another level called the postulating level where we begin to hold things tentative, where we begin to relate some new constructs and some new concepts to ourselves, and try to put new meaning into our concepts; and, there is a fifth level he calls the unifying stage, where you begin to have experiences and you ought to listen, he said, to those experiences you have. History, as he sees it, has developed that way, and living in 1971, we have all five breeds living together. Thus the difficulty. There are people still at the classifying stage. People still at the sensing stage, people still at the relating stage, where most of us are. And when we begin to talk about Black Economic Development, Black power all by itself, without being concerned about the larger social concern, we are at the relating level and we are not bringing about anything new and certainly no new changes.

I was talking to Dr. Bois one day, and I was insulted by what he said to me at first. Now I'm not saying he was right — I hope he was, when he explained what he meant. But as we were talking, we were talking about breeds of men and people who are in a special category and that sort of thing. People who thought differently, and perhaps better and more progressively had a greater responsibility. We were talking in general and we had been talking about Blacks at the same time — so I got all those things confused. He looked at me and said, "You have to be better than other people." Now you know that "bugged" me being from the South. I had been told that all my life. My grandmother told me I had to tie my tie and I had to have a clean shirt on and I resent all that now, because I want to be just as bad as other people or better, if I want to be, but I'd like to relate to me as well as I can. So when he said that to me, visions of the past and of old models came up. When he said to me, "You have to be better," I looked at him, I didn't say anything. I was disappointed in him because I had a lot of respect for him. And. then I thought about that and a week later I went back and I spoke to him again. I say, you know, you insulted me. He said, "How did I insult you?" I said you told me I have to be better than everybody else. Here I am on a so-called predominantly White faculty and why do I have to be better than they are? Why do I have to be better? Why can't I be just as good, why can't I go on and do my thing without being under the pressure of being better? I'm not relating to that any more. He looked at me and a tear welled up in his eye. He said, "Is that what you thought I said?" I replied "Yes, that's what I thought you said." He said, "I didn't mean that at all. I mean there are breeds of people on this earth. There are people who have a greater responsibility than other people because they have more, they have more vision, they see more things. I put you in that category." I liked what he said. I hope he was correct but I still have doubts about that. But putting myself out of the picture, he is correct, I think, about certain breeds being special with special responsibility.

He also made another statement. He said, "Do you know that the Black alienated person in this country has a better chance of bringing about basic changes here than the White man simply because the Black man feels alienated. He hasn't internalized the culture to the extent that the White has. Therefore, he should tap that creative experience he has there and bring about some changes. He has a responsibility for providing broad leadership, and not just in a particular area. I am talking about leaders of people and not leaders of a Black community or a White community. There are some young people coming along and there are some similar breeds of people who have this special kind of talent. They have tapped, or they have broken the creativity barrier, or they are trying to break it and therefore, they have an extra responsibility in that sense." Well that still was a pressure but it was a different kind of pressure.

Now, why do I see the need for broad concerns? Last night I was talking to a White friend of mine, who grew his hair long, and has a pretty wife. They went to Upstate New York, and they were refused service in a restaurant because he has long hair and the restaurant said they weren't serving any of those types. That bothered me. I couldn't believe it. Just as some White people don't believe that Black people receive this kind of treatment and worse. They can't believe it because it never happened to them. I couldn't believe what he was telling me. That hit me and I thought it was only one short step from genocide. These are the same people who support the war in

Vietnam. They believe that war is inevitable. I don't believe that; I reject that. They believe that man has no potential for remaking and making himself; that he is not in charge of himself; and they handle all of the conflicts in the same way. So, if we become marooned at a stage where we are just concerned about one community, then any kind of changes we bring about there, at that level, may be nullified by the larger community.

This summer I was in the Port Authority as a consultant. I gave up, half way through. They didn't know, that emotionally, I had given up, because I thought there was nothing I could do anyway. They were still using old mental constructs, old mental models in 1969. They were real horse and buggy types. There was no chance for communication. Typical statements would run like, "they all had nice short haircuts" and "they looked decent." Things of that sort. These were the kind of mental constructs that were coming out in 1969. And in these same people, you will notice there is a correlation between the position they hold to change, growth, social action and short or long haircuts. So we have to be concerned about the way things are done. There was a time when I wasn't concerned about the way people felt in Beverly Hills. Living on the periphery of Watts, I wasn't concerned, I was concerned about building my community. But I had a realization that I should not only be concerned about how my trash was being picked up but how well it was being picked up in Beverly Hills, too. Because, everything they think, what they think, what they feel, and what they do affects me. Their position gives us direction; because there is a relationship between all of us. They have no right to think any way they want about the direction in which we go. I have something to say about that wherever they are because I am concerned about me, my involvement, my future and the kind of progress we make. The reality of the situation is that we are involved in a very complex situation and as I deal with it more and more I begin to realize that we are involved in a process that transcends all of these boundaries that I am talking about.

Black Economic Development, in my judgment, whether we put up cooperatives, whether we put up government sponsored operations in the Black community, will not survive unless we do it with a universal outlook and with the idea that we are not only changing a Black community, but we are changing this nation; we are changing society. Otherwise it can be nullified — because there is just one short step between rejecting that fellow with the long hair and genocide against groups of people. Let's face it.

Now how do we prepare for these changes? What is our level of attack? Neil Postman, in this book, and McLuhan, has said it too, that the medium becomes a message. It doesn't matter whether we put a lot of substance in the classroom; don't get me wrong, we are concerned about substance in our teaching and that sort of thing, but if that substance hasn't got a process which speaks to growth and change and the building of a kind of theoretical process then we are still in trouble because we are not using some of the methods that will bring about change. We should worry less about the substance and more about the process that we are using. There is a book by Viktor Frankl, called *Man's Search for Meaning.* In this he said we've got our things all mixed up. We've become marooned at a low level. That many of the problems that we have are not just depressions, paranoia, etc., we all suffer from those kinds of things. It's not just schizophrenia or whatever you want to label it. We've marooned ourselves at a very low level by relating to ourselves in that manner. He founded a field called logotherapy, which is in opposition, somewhat, to psychotherapy. He said, "Most of the people who come to me are seeking a significance and a meaning in life and that when I begin to give them that significance and that meaning, when we begin to talk, when I begin to relate to them in that fashion, the other problems tend to disappear, that is, all of these psychological inabilities that they think they might have at that particular time." So I'm saying that man's search is for a greater meaning, something greater than he is, so we have to build. That overarching theoretical framework spoke about that emerges out of the how to do things, especially when we buy and commit ourselves to the concept of some kind of creativity.

In one of my classes, which was meeting at one of the students' homes, we were trying to discuss process. We weren't concerned about the substance. Everybody was turned off, everybody wanted to quit school. The University of Southern California is a middle-class school. These students were not relating to it. One student said "I'm not even going to pick up that degree." I could understand what they were talking about. This is a class on Urban Administration and Social Change, but I don't care if we ever really get there substantively. The point is can we relate to our students? Can we come out with some kind of creative person who can think about the new problems we are facing? It seems that this is what we are trying to build. Not filling their heads with a lot of knowledge about how to pave the streets that will come — but whether or not we have developed the creativity in people that can meet the new challenges we are facing. In this discussion, one of the Black students all of a sudden mentioned the word *love,* just like that. And he was saying "I could love Maddox. . . ." "I could love this man," he mentioned a lot of them, Southerners and Reagan. He said "I could love them," and this White fireman in there said "How could you love all those people?" Then he began to express it in these terms. He said, "In a broad kind of way, this is my value system, this is my overall theoretical frame of reference. This tells me how to operate in situations." He said, "For an example man, if you are with me when we walk in Watts, if you are really with me and you go down with me wherever you are, if you are really with me, nobody's going to bother you in Watts." And this fellow said, "I'm with you" — he sort of brought him into it. So it was a very moving kind of thing. He was using an old word in a new kind of way. Just a simple term love. We think about it in an erotic sense — a man and a woman — that's not necessarily what we are talking about. He's talking about, and I can see it when I talk about a new kind of epistemological framework; a theoretical framework, if you will, anything you want to call it — a new kind of construct — that enables us to see more and put things in their proper places; enables us to develop some new ideas about where we are going. So he used the word love and we all got silent — and that's another thing — we can't stand silence. We sat in the classroom and somebody spoke up and said, "Hasn't anybody got anything to say?" He had to break the silence — he could not live with that, on that level — where it really counts, where things were really happening. But anyway, that was his overarching kind of framework. He worked within that kind of love framework. We all have to have some personal construct, some overarching kind of framework. And I don't mean a thing that brings about decisions in toolbox fashion, but terms that emerge out of the *what*. If the *what* is actually defined well in terms of *where* we are going then out of that emerges the *how*. It does take time, however, but it emerges, eventually, if that *what* is well defined, and defined in terms of some of the new concepts I spoke of earlier, like man is a time-binder and not a space-binder.

I'm going to close on this note. We are all functionaries — people who perform duties. Nixon is a functionary for somebody. Wherever we are, we are functionary — we are functioning within a frame of reference. I am a functionary. We resent that somewhat; but we all are. We can classify functionaries into three types. We must recognize what kind of functionary we are. And once we recognize it, develop into becoming the kind of functionary we would like to be. The logical functionary, goes by the rule book — he doesn't develop any new vehicles; any new constructs. Everything that he is told to do, he does it. He doesn't question the legitimacy of anything. Secondly, there is the sociological functionary. He functions just a little bit differently. He does question a few things and he operates within the middle range theoretical frame of reference — he is concerned about organizations and how they function. And thirdly, there is the epistemological functionary. A guy who is looking, or a human who's looking, I don't want to leave the ladies out, a human who is looking for new ways of doing things — who will be a party to his own dismissal if he has to be. And he bases it on how he understands the world and how he has structured his world and his new constructs.

So I am saying that this overall frame of reference that we are talking about — a process — gives us a set of values, it becomes a vehicle and a methodology. I reject the survival model. The plant survives, we are talking about living, not just surviving. There is a difference when you begin to believe in your own potential. The survival of the fittest is the survival philosophy. The competitive philosophy is a survival philosophy: being a trustee for the next generation is a living philosophy because we don't own anything ourselves. We are just keepers until the next generation comes into being, then we pass it on in full blossom. When we become convinced that man can make and remake himself, then we will become more creative. We will transcend the normal boundaries and we will begin to relate to Black Economic Development as a process for developing new kinds of concepts and constructs, not just for Black people but for the whole of society and for this nation and give it some new direction.

CHAPTER XVI

SUMMARY AND POSTSCRIPT

Epistemics: A new process

I have in a spontaneous, discovering, creating, and inventing fashion immersed myself, as well as I could, in the formulation referred to as Modern General Semantics Epistemology; and, as well as I could at this time, related it specifically to the New Public Administration and in general to the areas of social science, education, etc. in a theoretic-pragmatic sense. My approach has been one of Process with specific emphasis on this as a method of inquiry.

I have alluded, also, to the new process of Epistemics which is now being invented, adapted, developed and applied, in general, under the pioneering of Dr. J. Samuel Bois — author of *Explorations In Awareness, The Art of Awareness, Communication as Creative Experience,* and *Breeds of Men,* and specifically, by (as far as I know) only Anthony Athos of The Harvard School of Business, Mark Liebig, Associate Director of the Institute of General Semantics at the University of Denver, and myself.

Now that I have given you the cosmetics, please allow me to say a few words about Epistemics as a new Process. In a special paper written in November of 1970, for presentation to some New York Educators entitled "Epistemics, A New Discipline," Dr. Bois outlines his interpretation of what the inventing of this new area means. He states:

"Those of us who have continued the work of Korzybski

(General Semantics Epistemology) have been for years in the ridiculous situation of people who claimed that we were dealing with improved methods of Communication, while we were unable to give to our own discipline a name that made sense to outsiders."

He continues his description by saying, in essence, that instead of restricting the notion of epistemology to a theory of intellectual knowledge — of which logic is the main part — it covers the general system of knowing, feeling, behaving, becoming and growing. It is an attempt to translate into a new formulation the whole range of man's activities — including the wisdom of the ages and make them as scientifically-artistic as possible with relevant Theoretic-Pragmatic application to the Arts, the Sciences — Social and Natural — Politics, Administration, person to person encounters, family life, education, transactions of all dimensions and whenever and wherever humans are functioning. Epistemics is based on Michael Foucault's Notion of Epistemology which is translated into a general system of knowing he refers to as episteme — in his book *Les Mots et Les Choses* — which is to be translated under the title of *The Order of Things* by Pantheon Books. Foucault, according to Bois, claims that in a culture, at a certain date, there is only *dominant* (the italics are mine) episteme and it determines the conditions that make possible any kind of knowing, whether it is expressed in *theories* or is silently embodied in *cultural* practices (italics are mine). Moreover, these general cultural practices and theories determine the patterns of how we speak, write, act, establish rules and set up our Permanent Institutions — Bois refers to this in his *Art of Awareness,* as our structural unconscious.

Thus, the formulation of Epistemics embraces: 1) Episteme as a direction, philosophy, and the way humans relate themselves to the world at a given time; 2) Epistemology as a science of knowing, i.e., the ways in which the sciences of humans are brought together in an organized fashion in sets of formulations, and postulations that bring a continuous revamping of our values, beliefs, modes of perceiving, feeling-thinking; and 3) General Semantics as methodology which uses the language as symbol and meaning making dimension as one way of penetrating and revising the old, inventing new symbols and language structures, new ways of perceiving ourselves, our culture and others; and, the how of practicing the skills of awareness and behaving which make us realize our potential for living and not merely surviving. In other words, the accumulated knowing through episteme and epistemology is put to use through the General Semantics Methodology. The three comprising epistemics give us a circular process and not a linear equation. In short, a way of developing a Cosmic Consciousness and translating that cosmic consciousness into transacting-process-like-action.

The long debate about whether or not General Semantics is relevant to or adequate for addressing the social concerns of our day is temporarily answered in the affirmative. At least the terminological and meaning problem has been advanced. Dr. Bois was anxious to give General Semantics a new name. He felt that the old name, as the question of why, has taken on a cultural bias that rendered it less powerful as a tool for managing our present day activities. It was my position, at the time he addressed the idea in a conversation and subsequently in a letter in reply to my position in Chapter XIII Toward A Unified Theory — A Theoretical Process (occasional paper number eight), that we should not discard the label of General Semantics; but, merely consider calling it Modern-up-to-date General Semantics Epistemology rather than just General Semantics, for fear of violating our own commitment to the General Theory of time-binding. I no longer hold that view. Epistemics covers what we do very well. It takes into consideration the cultural-environmental-cosmic and language dimensions that Korzybski referred to implicitly and somewhat explicitly in his book *Science and Sanity*. It does not, in my judgement violate the theory of time-binding. But, provides us with the orientation Korzybski was searching for in 1932-1933 when he played around with such terms as humanology, human engineering, General Theory or evolution and finally opted for General Semantics which name appeared to be satisfactory. Arthur Bentley, author of *The Knowing and the Known* along with John Dewey agreed with Korzybski as to the difficulty in finding an appropriate label. The two exchanged correspondence on the matter. In 1952 Bentley published an article in *Science* the weekly of A.A.A.S. entitled "Kinetic Inquiry" in which he too was wrestling with what he called the epistemological aspect of his work. The terminological problem was left in that state until November of 1970 when Bois came up with 'Epistemics' — a name that seems to make 'scientific' sense.

To me, Epistemics is not just a discipline but a process which differentiates between early General Semantics in a time-binding fashion as Quantum Mechanics is distinguished from the theory of relativity. It is a difference which makes a difference a *difference,* nothing is displaced, the overarching abstracting and multi-ordinal theories give us direction. In both instances effective time-binding is the correct basis for focusing. Again, to me, Epistemics is the quantum in the Social Sciences. It gives us a more powerful tool for observing. It is the movement from methods of simple observation or perception to scientific technology; finally, also, from scientific methods of Social Sciences to methods that include psychology, philosophy, interdisciplinary approaches, culturology, and epistemology; deriving its significance from all of the sciences of man. It is an ambitious program. But, if we are to take seriously the job of building a better world, staying in touch with the cosmos, relating to the emerging counter culture which Roszak talks about in *The Making of a Counter Culture,* the three levels of consciousness Charles Reisch talks about in *The Greening of America,* the New World of humankind outlined by Albert S. Szent-Gyorgyi in *The Crazy Ape* and the developing of the New Breeds referred to in *Breeds of Man* by Bois — we must relate to a quantum process of Epistemics which gives us new insight into the how of making the process not merely a diagnosis and prognosis tool; but, a way of postulating possibilities for realizing the ideals and goals of the New Direction. The quantum nature of Epistemics as a Process is one minor step in that direction. The first seven chapters of Bois' new manuscript as I interpret them, (still in process during 1971) moves us closer to the processes of the ongoing cosmos, a general system of knowing and not so much what and why but *how;* in a world where art, poetry, mathematics, religion, and science are interchangeable; and, innovating change and transformations are the warp and woof of every specific movement.

What makes this a difference which makes a difference a *difference?* In short, the basic premise of the formulation, is implicit and explicit, in the Epistemic Process and includes the non-verbal and cultural aspects of our local, world and cosmic environment — up to this point 1971. Before that, the General Semantics Formulation could not account for the microscopic and sub-microscopic behavioral characteristics that emerged in different cultural settings or societies operating within the Aristotelian Indo-European language tradition. There is an allness syndrome implicit in the notion that a new language structure imposed on a culture can bring about changes. It says, in other words, we are locked within the language and that change alone would make a significant difference — neglecting the fact that certain changes are occurring in certain societies, tied to the Aristotelian structure, and certain changes are not occurring in others — i.e., changes that speak to man as a human and effective time binder. Consequently, we must go beyond language to deal with factors that a revamped language structure does not touch, viz., cultural and implicit factors that emerge in spite of the kind of language being utilized. Therefore, the tentative conclusion is that the language is only one dimension and a formulation is needed which speaks to both the language and non-verbal factors that give direction to a developing humankind. The Epistemic approach gives us that orientation. It includes the General Semantics notion and 'opens the door' for the inventing of methodologies which address the silent postulates of emergence and transformation. This is a difference which makes a difference a *difference* — and, it is an orientation; a dimension which speaks to process, the formative tendency of our world, and evolution of humankind.

The most powerful instrument employed to this date to implement this new dimension and epistemic process is the epistemological profile. Invented by Bachelard in his *Philosophy of No* and reorganized with new inventions by J. Samuel Bois, I postulate the epistemological profile as a tool and method for bringing into existence the New Epistemic Process.

Epistemics does two things: one, it incorporates the General Semantics formulation — which is concerned more with individual and group personal growth, emergence and transformation; second it provides a new way of perceiving these individuals and groups within their cultural settings; along with an evaluation of that cultural setting and the non-verbal factors that play such an important part relative to total direction, emerging and transforming. Specifically, Epistemics speaks directly to the question of the relevancy of the General Semantics formulation, and the Epistemic Process, for not only comprehending individual change; but, dramatic, radical and revolutionary social change.

This is a partial answer to the questions raised by Anatol Rapaport at the International Conference on General Semantics in 1968 when he said: (and I paraphrase) General Semantics has failed in dealing with massive social and radical change in our systems and institutions, (see for further details, Lee Thayer, *Communication: A General Semantic Perspective* — Spartan Books, pp. 163-176). He received these replies: one by Allen Walker Read who maintained that the right of revolution is inherent when conventional means have failed; but, he felt that we had to reject the posture of despair in that General Semantics is not a cause but a discipline drawing upon the best scientific methods for the deep restructuring of human beings to make optimal use of their potentialities, (see Lee Thayer, *Communication: A General Semantic Perspective,* pp. 176-180 for further details). Another reply was from D. Daniel Bourland, Jr. who said he thought the relevance would lie in working with small groups of leaders in strategic positions using General Semantics methodology embedded in a semantic context of time binding, (for further details see Lee Thayer, *Communi-*

cation: A General Semantics Perspective, pp. 180-183). Bois in his reply in *Breeds of Men,* said he did not hold much for General Semantics as the Savior of the world as originally conceived. His hope lies in developing new methods which speak to the dramatic issues of the day. And, that all we could do would be to continue developing; and, that his *Breeds of Men* was just one experiment in that direction, (see J. Samuel Bois, *Breeds of Men,* Chapter 16, Harper and Row). Thus, I see the question of Epistemics as another step in the direction of developing methods of relevance for restructuring, revamping and revolutionizing our institutions, systems, society and humankind. It contains the spirit and method for devising a blueprint for change.

Epistemics is a philosophy and method of courage; a process ushering in a new era and dimension to the change process; the making of a new kind of human; and most of all putting an end to 'Sham.'

Gardner Murphy alludes to this when he speaks of a coming 'third human nature;' Korzybski speaks of a 'new kind of man;' Bachelard speaks of 'mental mutations:' Bridgeman sees it as the beginning of a cultural or conceptual revolution; Bois speaks of 'Breeds of Men;' Whyte speaks of the formative tendency of the Cosmos; and I speak of an Overarching Framework enabling us to travel to a high level of abstraction and penetrate the very depths of the Change Process.